INSIDE OUT

By
Carl McMurray

© SPIRITBUILDING, 2004, All Rights Reserved. No part of this book may be reproduced in any form without the written permission of the publisher. Printed in the United States of America.

Helping build your spirit for the contest of life.

www.spiritbuilding.com for more tracts and study helps

SPIRITBUILDING PUBLISHING
15591 N. State Rd. 9, Summitville, Indiana, 46070

COVER PHOTO: Denali National Park, Alaska.
By Carl McMurray

Table of Contents   Page

WHY IS THIS A NEEDED STUDY?...............................	4
A DIRECTED SPIRIT...	11
A CONFIDENT SPIRIT...	19
A FIERY SPIRIT..	29
A PRAYERFUL SPIRIT..	40
A COMMITTED SPIRIT...	52
A SHARING SPIRIT..	67
AN ENCOURAGING SPIRIT..................................	77
A LOVING SPIRIT..	87
A STEADFAST SPIRIT...	100
A UNIFIED SPIRIT...	110
A THANKFUL SPIRIT...	120

LESSON 1   WHY IS THIS STUDY NEEDED?

A new birth is an exciting time. Parents and grandparents are thrilled at what they have done, what has been given them, and what lies before them. Our cup runs over with hopes and dreams flowing from the potential of this new son or daughter. The future holds many different roads that can be traveled, however. The one we want our children to walk, of course, is the one where they grow into obedient, mannerly, deeply spiritual adults. We want them to be hard workers with complete educations who know how to make time for the beautiful woman or wonderful man they find and choose to marry, while at the same time being fully committed to the Lord and His kingdom. There are other paths that are walked in the future though. Sometimes there is tragedy as a young life is lost to illness or accident. And sometimes we learn to just "make do" in life because our children (or we) never grasp the full potential of a talent or education which was within their reach.

A spiritual birth is like the above. There is a time for rejoicing and excitement and zeal and intense effort on behalf of the "young one." Teachers and those influencing the "birth" feel proud and excited about their part. There is education and activity ahead to help him/her develop and mature, but then something happens. Sometimes it is tragedy as a spiritual disease (such as jealousy, regret, covetousness, or lust) finds a home and kills the child of God. More often, however, what happens is much like life itself. The child of God simply reaches a spiritual plateau. He may decide he is just like everyone else so there is no more need to press forward. Perhaps he comes to understand he will never be completely perfect, so he might as well stop trying. Whatever the reason, one's potential is never fully reached, zeal dies, and growth either stops or slows so as to become immeasurable. Attendance at worship may be regular and the desire to go to heaven is still present, but worship itself often becomes a hollow exercise without any real joy or excitement. Interest in the Scriptures begins to wane and Bible classes seem pointless. More and more often we will begin to hear faultfinding and complaining rather than praising and giving thanks. And it is truly sad when we realize that this grumbling is coming from our own lips.

I don't know how it got started, but there is a gesture I noticed being used by the Russians when I was over there which describes the above spiritual situation in the lives of many. When faced with problems they believed to be insurmountable the Russians would hold up their hands, shrug their shoulders, and ask, "What's to do?" then go about their business. Whatever the task was that needed to be done would be simply dropped, no matter how important or time sensitive the task. It would be treated as some kind of impossible mission. I'm afraid that we might be as fatalistic as Russians in this area. We know there's a problem, we feel something is lacking, but we don't really see much answer in those around us. We don't know what to do ourselves so we spiritually shrug our shoulders, determine nothing can be done and go about our business. How sad for us, for those we could influence, and for the church of Jesus Christ.

The answer is right in front of us if we will but look and see. Our zeal, our interest, our excitement, and our joy in being children of God was/is greatest when we're growing. When we were changing, learning, and practicing our new faith – it had a great deal of meaning for us. When we first saw our brethren as helpers, partners, and family members, we would have bitten our tongue off rather than complain or find fault with them. When we get back to "growing" then our spiritual lives will get back to "going." We will not be able to sit still on our plateau. Just as it is almost impossible for a healthy child to sit still (they simply have too much energy, curiosity, etc.), likewise the growing Christian will find it difficult to be apathetic, bored, and mediocre about things. He won't be able to sit still; life simply holds too many opportunities that must be explored now.

TWO CONSIDERATIONS ON GROWING

There are two aspects to Christian growth that I believe are important for us to notice and think about. First, have you noticed that most of the personal changes that we make in our lives are made when we are young? I would suspect that most of us change more from age 10 to 20 than we do the rest of our lives. When we "settle down" in the physical world, it becomes difficult to make changes. The responsibility of a job, a spouse, children, etc. may force us to continue walking in the path we have chosen. Not so, spiritually. One wonderful aspect of growth in Christ is that it can be "jump started" at any time. We may go through periods of staleness and discouragement, but we don't have to stay there. There is no indication that Peter was addressing himself simply to young Christians when he wrote his two epistles. Quite the contrary in fact. Yet in both letters he exhorts them to grow.

In 1 Peter 2:1-3 his directions are in the context of putting away the attitudes of this life that actually inhibit growth. These are attitudes like malice (an evil spirit toward another), deceit, hypocrisy, envy, and slander. These sinful heart diseases act like cancers to the child of God, halting healthy growth and weakening the system for other diseases. Peter encourages his readers to "long for the pure milk of the word, so that by it you may grow in respect to salvation." In a garden, weeds and pests must be removed as well as water, light, and fertilizer added for the plant to grow. In growing a child we surely consider food, exercise, rest, and study as necessities. But we must also give care that dangers are avoided and hygiene followed to avoid disease. So it is with spiritual growth. There are things to add that will help us toward spiritual health (we hope that some of these are the subjects of this book) and there are things that must be put away so that growth is not hindered. Peter he says put this first list away so that you can focus on the second, the directions to be found in the word.

In his second letter the apostle closes with the admonition to be on guard and not carried away from the faith, 2 Peter 3:17-18. The best way to be in this condition seems to be for them to be growing in the grace and knowledge of the Saviour. This is an interesting turn of phrase because the two are actually intertwined. We cannot grow in grace and ignorance. Likewise, we should not grow in knowledge without making changes that make us more Christlike, i.e. appropriating more grace or favor (as Jesus himself grew in God's favor, according to Luke 2:52). Our conclusion then is that we grow in grace when, and while, we grow in the knowledge of our Lord. Again we note

...Growth in New Testament churches *page 7*

that it is not to new Christians that Peter sends this admonition, but to those who are "scattered," i.e. to Christians all over Turkey who were there either because that was their home, or more likely, because they had been persecuted and forced to flee their homelands for less civilized areas. These servants of God may have been discouraged and even fearful at times, yet the Holy Spirit's directions for them was to keep defeating the world, be on their guard, and grow. This same admonition would apply in any age and it certainly applies in ours today.

The second important thing to see here is that this growth never really needs to stop in this life. Yes, we let it stop, if we're not paying attention to warnings like Peter's. And the Devil is certainly always looking for ways to distract us from spiritual things and get us caught up in the things of this life. In fact, he is so effective at it that he doesn't even see the need to update his tool chest. 1 John 2:15-17 lists the three main distractions that the Devil uses. He used all three on Eve at the beginning. He used them to lead the Israelites into the sin of grumbling. He used them to weaken the Kings and rulers of Judah. He even tried the same tricks on Jesus as our Lord began his ministry and he finally ran into one wise enough to see through the deception and say "no" to the temptations. But it doesn't have to be this way. It is not decreed in the unchanging heavens that we must stop growing. What can be fantastic to us if we develop the right attitude is that every time we learn something, God can provide us a new way to use this knowledge and expand the experience of learning. There is no end to the experiences and opportunities, which are available to us, if we will make ourselves available to God. Growth doesn't have to stop, but if it does it can be started again! Isn't the grace of God a marvelous thing as he provides for our needs in this life?

Paul noted that the outward man is definitely decaying day by day, in 2 Corinthians 4:16, but the same verse tells us our inner selves should be "renewed" in the same time period, that is, day by day. Our prayer in this study should be for inner renewal. For the growth that lends to us the youthful exuberance and energy of spirit which rightfully belongs to every child of God. Let me note just a few things that are natural to the environment of growth, things which should probably be noticed in our lives also, day by day.

When a family grows, i.e., a couple has children, there are several things involved in the ideal situation. I know that not all physical families will go through this because sometimes people become parents by surprise and sometimes even when it is not a surprise some people just haven't put the thoughtfulness and prayer into their family situation that they should have. In the area of spiritual growth however, we can think this thing out and act in accordance with wisdom if we wish. No one is born accidently into the kingdom of God and the same concern and thought that moves one to this place can move one in a continual motion of progress if that is his or her desire. Consider a few things that will add strength and depth to our purposing in ourselves to grow...

Desire. We've already looked at Peter's words where he instructs the child of God to "long for" the word and resulting growth. Although sadly, sometimes one is born into a family where no child was desired. That is not so with God's family. The physical child must struggle to grow in such a dark environment. The spiritual child however is under no such compulsion. If he loses his desire to grow, he simply stops and dies, quietly and sometimes unnoticed. The Christian must continually work on his desire to grow.

Planning. Wise parents think about children before they ever arrive. It has been said that parents who wait until a child is born to talk about training and discipline have already waited 9 months too long. Likewise the forward thinking Christian will not just drift along and leave his growth to chance. He will plan for it by feeding himself properly, taking advantage of opportunities to be with other Christians and study together and read on his own. He will exercise himself by trying new activities, volunteering his assistance, getting involved in the work of the local family of God, and fellowshipping with brethren. There are too many other ways that an individual can see to his own growth to mention here. Perhaps sharing some of your own ideas in a class setting would be an encouragement to others.

Communication. In a family wise mates communicate, parents need to communicate with children, and vice versa. In the church of God Christians need to be talking up, talking over, and talking with one another. We need to be praising one another, talking down sin, and encouraging the faint hearted and struggling. There are too many congregations where hard questions are discouraged and even rebuked and suggestions are simply ridiculed. Any eldership that discourages open communication and fails to be open itself in all their decisions and leadership roles commits some grievous errors. First, they're failing to model leadership to the flock and therefore failing in their role of maturing more leaders. This is why in many congregations there are whole generations of men unfit for leadership. They were never matured spiritually. Secondly, they are encouraging a sense of frustration and stifling growth that has been seen in many cases to end in great explosions in the congregation where some young Christian or faint hearted one may become discouraged and even turn from the faith. At the very best these ugly divisions hurt the cause of Christ in the area where the church is located, sometimes for years to come. Spiritual scars remain for decades. Many times this could have been avoided if we had just troubled ourselves to communicate.

Work. Many times throughout the New Testament we are told to be "diligent." That is, we are to put forth effort. Growth is no different from any other responsibility in that way, it will take effort. It takes effort to communicate, effort to plan, effort to grow. That translates in our world as time and/or money, two very precious commodities. Ephesians 4:16 teaches us however that the body grows from that which every joint supplies. The supplying of your effort will go a long way in bringing the congregation that you identify with as family, to maturity and effectiveness.

There are many volumes on the book shelves today dealing with church growth and that subject is certainly important. But the real key to church growth, this author believes, is individual growth. When a congregation is full of spiritually healthy Christians who love one another deeply and show it, who practice their faith outside the walls of their local assembly halls and demonstrate the character of Christ in their daily walk then the growth of the local congregation will be a moot point, not even worthy of discussion. The world will line up at the door when Christians start waking up and living like they really believe they are going to heaven and they want everyone to go with them. God bless your studies.

QUESTIONS ON LESSON ONE

1. What are some things that might lead a Christian to "level off" in his or her spiritual growth?

2. What is usually the time of greatest growth for the Christian? Why?

3. List three things that you believe hinder spiritual growth and please explain the dynamic behind each that causes the hindrance.

4. Name the three tools that Satan uses to separate us from God, and please give an actual example of how each one works.

5. Please give three things that you believe will encourage spiritual growth. The ideas given in the lesson are fine, but see how many others you can come up with.

6. What four things are absolutely necessary to personal spiritual growth?

7. What dangers can arise when communication lines are not open?

...Growth in New Testament churches *page 11*

A DIRECTED SPIRIT — LESSON 2

This is a true story. An "apathy club" was started on a certain university campus a few years ago. Officers of the club advertised a meeting, and guess what! No one showed up for the meeting. All the members were too apathetic to care about attending.

Apathy is defined as a lack of feeling or emotion, impassiveness, lack of interest or concern. When apathy sets in, the next step is mediocre work and complacent attitudes. It is a close cousin to self-satisfaction and thrives on excuses and rationalization. It may be humorous as a club, but it drains the vitality of Christ's body. Consider the efforts in your local congregation. Has this problem crept into the Bible studies, the preaching, or the singing? Is it gaining footholds in others aspects of our worship and/or work such as the Lord's supper, our giving, our benevolence or visiting? It can be seen in boring worship services, lack of interest in studies, little association between Christians, declining budget figures, and a lack of goals or planning for the future.

Growth Leads To Confidence Leads To Growth

There is a remedy for apathy that is found in growth. Growth is movement in a specific direction, i.e., up! What a wonderful word God has chosen to describe becoming more like Him. Mentally and spiritually one simply cannot be growing and apathetic at the same time.

Athletics are often used in Scriptures as a figure of the active Christian. They are a good parallel because of the energy, the drive, and the commitment the athlete must give to his chosen sport. They are also a good figure because the athlete must "grow" in his sport to compete. As he grows in his sport, he gains confidence and with increased confidence and interest, apathy is pushed back. He overcomes mental as well as physical barriers to continue his competition. This principle is true in hunting, football, martial arts, investing in commodities, anything, even our spirituality. When we grow in anything, our confidence rises. As our confidence level goes up, so does our interest.

And when interest goes up, apathy goes down in flames.

Naturally the next question is, "How do we go about growing?"

Recognizing The Need To Grow

Spiritual growth differs from physical growth in a major respect. It is a choice! The little child who eats and plays has no choice; he is going to grow up. The child of God is different. He must choose to grow and mature. He must choose to eat and exercise spiritually. He can exist for a long time on a starvation diet, being miserable and making others this way also, or he can choose to nourish himself and mature. Recognizing this need is the very first step in the process.

Hebrews 6 gives us the divine expectation for God's children, that is, they are expected to press on to maturity – to grow! Verses 4-8 give us warning about condemnation awaiting those who don't grow. If we don't mature, you see, we are dying. Now notice verse 9. The writer expresses confidence in them that they can do this; growth is not asking the impossible.

2 Peter 3:17-18 encourages us to grow in order to be on our guard and not carried away by error. Timothy was told by Paul that his growth should be so visible that his "progress may be evident to all," 1 Timothy 4:15.

When we begin to see the danger in not growing (Hebrews 5:11-14) which threatens us, and the definite desire of God for all His children to mature, then we are beginning to move in the right direction. When we begin to understand the church of Jesus Christ can only grow when "I" grow (Ephesians 4:12, 15-16), so Jesus who loves me is really waiting on "me" in order to get busy doing His work, then we are beginning to understand the importance of this subject and the need for personal application.

The Need For Direction

The tallest building is only as powerful as its foundation. A plant is completely dependant on its root system. A map is close to useless without knowing one's present location. Growth is like this also. We need to know where we are and what our lives are built upon. God's word is our compass. It will point the way for us, but we must trust it and move in that direction.

There can be no movement without settling on a direction. One who aims at nothing will hit it every time. One who plans to go nowhere will get there at a record pace.

The following are several directions, listed in Rubel Shelly's, "Going on to Maturity," which can help us get started on the right course.

Burn Your Bridges Behind You. That is, make a clean break with activities and people that are a sinful influence on your life. Someone on a diet needs to stay out of candy stores just as the alcoholic must avoid his old drinking buddies. Romans 6:2, 6 talks about putting the old man of sin to death in our lives. That's how evil influences must be dealt with. If you don't want to be hindered by the complaining faultfinder or gossip, then you must break off with them. Worldly friends and activities, which pull us away from spirituality, will stunt or even kill one's growth, Matthew 13:22. 2 Corinthians 7:10 tells us that sorrow for sin, which is true and according to the will of God, will produce a repentance without regret. There can be no looking back or making plans for failure.

Grow In The Knowledge Of God. The Christian should have a little time daily that he/she spends in God's word. Peter calls this desire for knowledge a "longing," 1 Peter 2:2. Jesus said this knowledge is the key for true freedom (John 8:31, 32), and part of this freedom is the freedom to grow up in Christ. God's word is our Creator actually speaking to us, giving us direction. The facts that are written are important, but don't neglect to look for the application to be made in your life. Open classes where Bible passages are discussed can be helpful in this regard.

Keep The Lines Of Communication Open. That is, pray without ceasing, 1 Thessalonians 5:17. This short passage implies our prayers should be regular, continual, and habitual. Profitable prayer like everything else requires discipline, forethought, and even scheduling sometimes. If you want to grow, however, this is a must.

Fellowship. The Lord's body is a "sharing together," a partnership. Every single member needs the encouragement that comes from being part of this family. Drug addicts and alcoholics recognize their need for support groups, such as NA and AA. We need to humble our thinking to realize we need our support group also, for our addiction to sin and this world. Hebrews 10:25 encourages us to make meeting with the saints a dedicated part of our life. Whenever the doors are open, we should be striving to be present. Let me briefly encourage each one to participate in more than just public worship assemblies, however. Worship has been described as being like a restaurant where all kinds of people meet, sit down together, and then part without knowing or caring about each other. Growth requires more than this. It requires real relationships and caring. This can be encouraged through small group studies, recreational activities, and close friendships with other believers which all go together to build strong ties of love and partnership in the Lord's work.

Win Others To Christ. A pure life, Bible study, prayer, and fellowship will all help to equip one as he moves toward the goal of soul-winning, but this is actually our task. Ignoring this part of our growth is like going to college and then retiring after our graduation. We are like finely tuned race cars, which never leave the garage. Saving the lost was the task of our Savior (Luke 19:10), and He is our example, 1 Peter 2:21. We too should be saving the lost.

> **"The average member of the church of Christ has heard 4,000 sermons, sung 20,000 songs, participated in 8,000 public prayers...and converted zero sinners."**
> (Hearts on Fire, a Strategy for Dynamic Evangelism by Don Humphrey)

What would you think of a restaurant where the manager showed up to let all the kitchen help come to work, then locked the doors while they spent all day feeding each other? Some congregations are like this, I'm afraid, because they have lost their direction. This is a strong indication that growth has ceased or is close to ceasing, and it is only the individual workers who can change and do better. The world simply cannot be saved without hearing the good news of Christ and this is your job and mine. This is the plan of God, Romans 10:14; 1 Corinthians 1:20-25. This is what we are growing toward, as well as being part of the growth process itself.

Convinced or Converted

We know we need to grow and we basically know the directions on how to bring this growth about. So the question still must be asked, why aren't we growing? Why do so many Christians feel stale and left behind in their spiritual lives? Why is our worship in many areas seemingly empty and devoid of any real joy and praise? The answer might be found in understanding the difference between the terms – convinced and converted.

A few years ago a brother in central Florida visited a number of sound and faithful congregations in the state. He took his family and visited churches where he was not known or recognized. His findings were quite revealing. Of the numerous congregations he visited, only one welcomed him and invited him back. In every one his children were late for class because no one offered to help them find their classes. Not a single invitation of hospitality was extended. One has to ask…were the people in these congregations convinced or converted, i.e., were they converted into servants of the Lord and committed to doing His will? Or were they just convinced by facts, that being "at church" was the right thing so they were doing their part by attending. There is a vast difference between being convinced and being converted, and this difference will influence whether we are able to grow up into Christ or not.

The Convinced Person

The convinced person believes and accepts a set of facts. They are necessary, but not urgent. He does not have a devastating awareness of his past sinfulness, thus he feels no sense of rescue from death or deliverance. Feelings mean little to this person and he may even object to religious feelings. To this one, faith is a matter of possessing the proper facts and building a few "necessary" habits. Once this habit of lifestyle is accepted the person settles into a "normal" life and assures himself all is right with his life because he has accepted the right facts. His life will often seem comfortable and simple and he simply cannot comprehend his own sinfulness or the seriousness of accountability and eternal condemnation. Scheduling recreation activities around regular worship services may be about the maximum spiritual effort this individual has to offer.

The Converted Person

This person is a stark contrast to the former. Being converted hurts. It is not simple or easy, but it certainly is worth it to lay hold of the great blessings, which are offered. This one acknowledges condemnation as just punishment for sin. Sin hurts him, whether it is in him or others and forgiveness is a refreshing stream. Being converted is life shattering. It is awaking from the daze of thinking that we control our lives to the reality of sin controlling us. It is seeing that we are not "OK" with God, but offensive to Him in our attitudes and actions. It is knowing that God loves us deeply so that WE MUST change.

Being converted involves fear. There is a fear of judgment, fear of where we're going and how close we are, fear which is strong enough to make us change course and repent, often in tears. Repentance involves many hard choices, but fear forces us to go forward.

Being converted is finding the Savior. It is a small taste of holiness and real purity. It is an overwhelming tide of forgiveness, acceptance, and love. One's quiet life is destroyed. Conversion involves the whole man – mind and heart, knowledge and emotions, body and soul. It is more than a list of facts, which are accepted. It is renewal!

Why Do We Hinder Our Growth By Remaining Unconverted?

There may be several reasons for this. One may be simply misunderstanding. It is possible to substitute being "in the church" for being "in Christ." Although actually these terms may overlap, spiritually they are miles apart. Perhaps some are answering the wrong question when they ask, "Have I been baptized?" instead of "Have I really made Jesus Christ Lord of my life?" This is that "to do" list mentality rather than giving ourselves over to the Lord.

Another reason is many do not want to be converted. Some come to church and do not come to Christ at all. They never do change their lives, thoughts, emotions, goals, nothing changes. They are more interested in

...Growth in New Testament churches

"belonging to a church" than in "serving" as a Christian. Such ones will never be able to grow up into Christ because they have not come to the Lord in the first place. Unlike the prodigal son, they never do "come to themselves" and see the pigpen of sin which they live in. Sin never becomes terrible to them so they simply never develop a strong desire for the Father's love and commendation.

As long as we remain convinced without being converted, our spiritual growth will suffer. One's heart must be part of the growth process as much as one's head. When we come to appreciate our own need for growth, as well as the fact we have been given a compass for direction, then the natural reaction will be to head off in the proper direction. If we will not resist that guiding force, then growth will be as natural in the spiritual realm as in the physical.

QUESTIONS ON LESSON TWO

1. What is one of the main dangers facing Christians in this age today?

2. What is the obvious cure?

3. What is a major difference between physical growth and spiritual?

4. What is the "divine expectation?"

5. Is growth something that is visible or invisible? How much so?

6. What is the key to the church growing?

7. What are 5 basic "first-steps" in growth?

8. How shall we deal with evil influences?

9. Name a way in which we can plan to fail.

10. Name some "methods" which can help us grow in knowledge.

11. How has worship been described? What are your feelings about this?

12. What is a "convinced" person?

13. What is a "converted" person?

14. What one point in this lesson stands out to you as being one worthy of remembering?

A CONFIDENT SPIRIT — LESSON 3

Victor Sobrikoff quit school when he was 15. His grades were poor and failing. He had been told, by both parents and teachers, he was just plain dumb. For the next 18 years he lived by washing dishes and holding dead end jobs without ever being able to really see a direction in his life. At age 33 one job interview in his long list of interviews required an IQ test which subsequently revealed Victor's IQ was 161. His life changed. He quit being a bum, and in the remainder of his life turned into a writer, an inventor, as well as a prominent businessman. What made the difference in this man's life? Only that someone finally told him he was not dumb, he was smart. Someone he believed in (in this case an objective test) told him he could and he should! With this confidence, he did!

I Have Good News And Bad...

This true account illustrates a principle which most of us understand, as long as we apply it to someone else, that is. We seem to have more trouble with self-analysis for some reason. The principle is the same one Solomon describes in proverb form in Proverbs 23:7, "for as he thinks within himself, so is he." The principle we're talking about is based in human nature and says we will usually be what we think we are. A person will rise no higher than he believes he can within himself. One will simply not accomplish those things that he/she believes are impossible to accomplish. However, this is just the good news. You may rightly ask, "Why is this good news, that I limit myself by my thinking?"

It is good news because the other side of the coin is we also free ourselves by our thinking. We can encourage ourselves and reach previously unexpected heights. A person can either set his own limits or develop an unlimited potential. As Christians we should be vitally interested in tapping into the latter.

Many athletes have learned the benefits of "visualizing." This is nothing more than removing whatever barriers stand between them and victory, in their minds, over and over again until they are convinced they can complete their task. The pole-vaulter imagines each step down his approach, setting his pole and smoothly going up and over the bar. The martial artist goes over each move in his form, watching closely with his mind's eye. Every shift in balance or snap of the wrist is studied in his mind until he is convinced he will do the exercise perfectly. Many different disciplines use this simple approach to "see" and convince themselves that they not only "can" accomplish their goals, they "will." Consciously or unconsciously they have accepted Solomon's principle and are using it to their advantage. They have realized that as we think within ourselves, so we will be!

But remember, it is God who said this through Solomon, not some athletic coach. The power, which is available in a confident attitude, was set into our minds and hearts by a Creator who desires all men to come to Him, 2 Peter 3:9. This power of a changed attitude then finds its highest and noblest achievement, not on the tracks and fields of our universities, but in the race we run against sin and the fights we enter into with Satan. It is in the life we lead day by day, and in the changes of heart and character which can be accomplished with years of loving commitment, where we really begin to see God's power to help us grow into our full potential.

But What's The Bad News?

If God has blessed us with the power to do and be more than we originally believed, then where's the bad news? The answer is the unhappy part of this principle of confidence and has to do with where this powerful confidence is placed. Let me explain.

Romans 10:17 tells us that faith comes from hearing the word of Christ. Paul is speaking of a personal, motivating, saving faith. You may have many personal beliefs, but the inner trust in God and the saving power of His Son which motivates one to obedience comes from hearing (i.e., receiving) God's word. The more we hear (understand and accept) then the more one's faith in the word will grow. The principle is also true of error, however. We can develop faith in men's teaching from repeated exposure. If we listen continually and keep giving consideration to false teaching, especially linked with the desire to believe, there is no limit to the extremes of error which men are capable of accepting. Thus the admonition by the Spirit in Philippians 4:8-9 to let our mind dwell only on those things which are true, honorable, right, pure, lovely, and of good reputation. And our spiritual practices should be based upon the example of the apostles. My point is that we will develop a stronger faith in whatever we hear and receive into our hearts whether it is truth or error. This is because "faith comes by hearing."

Our confidence works in much the same way. It is true we will usually be able to accomplish whatever we think we can accomplish. Our problem is that we often use the opinions of others, or even our own fears, as the basis for setting our own personal level rather than the actual facts of our God given abilities and opportunities. The child who is often called "dumb" or "bad" will usually act this way. Is this because it's true? Not usually, rather it's because he has been convinced that he/she is this way. He will be what he thinks he is in his heart. Most wise parents understand this and attempt to build self-esteem in their children by complimenting them and teaching them about the possibilities that are available. Our heavenly Father does the same. He points out to His children the different dangers which can trip them up, encourages them as individuals to explore their own personal talents, and reassures them that His love will always be there to help and sustain them.

We Are Faced With A Bully

Part of our problem with growing in confidence is when we allow ourselves to be intimidated. We are listening all right. But we are listening to the wrong ones and getting a false picture of ourselves and of our abilities.

In the second grade life became difficult for me. I was faced with the first person I can remember who didn't seem to need any reason to pinch, push, or otherwise physically and verbally attack me. I don't fear second graders too much anymore (unless they start grouping together), but at the time I was in a miserable state. It took some convincing, but finally my mother persuaded me that the best thing I could do would be to ball up my fist and plant it on his nose as hard as I could. The day came when my mother's convictions in me and the class bully went head to head. I remember thinking this was the moment Mom had been talking about. Today I don't remember the actual events that triggered the situation, but I sure do recall swinging my fist. I remember it clearly because my tormenter was not only strong, he was fast. I swung, he ducked, and I was introduced to Florida Pine bark. That was the end of my first fight.

If you were thinking here that this experiment failed miserably, you'd be wrong. A couple of lessons come through loud and clear. First of all, I started learning not to be afraid. Nothing that young fellow did to me in second grade hurt as much as socking that pine tree. He didn't seem too tough anymore. Secondly, even though I missed him, he never bothered me anymore. That's how bullies often are, you see. The proper resistance was all it took to send him away. A full-fledged beating was unnecessary.

That's how it is with Christians sometimes. We are faced with a bully. Peter calls him a "roaring lion" in 1 Peter 5:8. He loves to frighten and intimidate his prey with his loud noise. To be sure, he will devour us if he is allowed to do so, but we don't have to let him. Revelation 20:4-6 speaks of the thousand-year reign of our Lord Jesus Christ. Verses two and three speak of Satan being bound for that same period of time. While Jesus reigns, Satan is bound. He simply cannot take a child of God by force. Like a second grade bully, James promises us that if we will "resist the Devil he will flee from you." We don't have to give him a beating; God will take care of that. All we have to do is resist him.

A Flanking Attack – Mistaken Ideas

Satan can't force us to fall; however, he is still not helpless. He can sap the strength of his prey by the fearfulness of his roar. If we are not careful, we can hear his noise and lose confidence. The devil has several "confidence killers" which he uses frequently and which many people have accepted. Here are a few.

God doesn't use "common" folk! What a strange idea for people to have who claim to follow the words of some freshwater fishermen. Fishing was one of the most "common" activities of that time and yet here is where Jesus went to specifically choose His special band of messengers who were going to be trained and given the most important task in history, that of taking the good news of a savior into the whole world. What, besides "common"

...Growth in New Testament churches page 23

folk can you see in God's choice of a shepherd and fig picker in the prophet Amos? Matthew was a tax collector and Simon was a political fanatic, sworn enemies, yet serving on the same team. What of the first king of Israel? He was so shy that he hid in the baggage at his coronation. We could go on and on, but the fact should be clear, God doesn't not use "common" folk. He especially uses "common" folk, because this where He gets the glory.

One must have extraordinary talents to be useful to God. Daniel and three other teenage boys didn't seem extraordinary until the test came and they simply put their faith in God. These boys, along with Nehemiah, Ezekiel, and Esther, were people in a foreign land, in captivity, dominated by powerful and sometimes bloody kings. The only thing which really could have been extraordinary about them was their determined attitude to be faithful. They all seemed to have been confident in their God, that everything would be OK if they just remained faithful. We don't need extraordinary talents to serve God – we just need to hang in there and follow His instructions, letting Him do what He does best.

> **GOD HAS CREATED EACH OF US AS EXTRAORDINARY PEOPLE IF WE WILL SIMPLY USE WHAT HE HAS GIVEN US.**

Extraordinary people are extraordinarily rare. This is another lie from the Devil and, like most of his lies; it is just a twisted truth. As evidenced by the rising rate of illegitimate births and the terrible divorce rate in our nation – committed and dedicated people are becoming rare finds. That's not to say they aren't out there, they are. They just don't get the public notice they deserve, so, when we run across one, he/she often surprises us. But the truth is that God has created each of us as extraordinary people if we will simply use what He has given us.

The average person reads 250-300 words per minute. Some have raised this level to two thousand to five thousand words per minute. That's extraordinary. Some people can stand at the door of a meeting room greeting visitors and later recall over 300 names from those short introductions. That also is extraordinary. What's really interesting here is that the above characters teach others how to do the same thing in their seminars.

It's been said that we only really use about 5% of the mental capacity we are blessed with, the rest of our gray matter just sits there. Albert Einstein wasn't so kind. He estimated the figure at closer to .02%. Extraordinary people are not rare, but people who will commit themselves completely to a cause and stick with it to the best of their abilities are. This should be a description of every "Christian."

We must stop listening to the world and its ruler. Jesus said he is a murderer, a liar, and the father of lies, John 8:44. The apostle Paul called him a schemer (2 Corinthians 2:11) who wants to take advantage of us, but we know how he works. We don't have to be deceived. Listen to God. He knows us better than we know ourselves. When the devil whispers in our ear and says, "You can't," God shouts from heaven and says, "You Can!"

God Says "You Can"

Over and over in the Scriptures we are assured of what God can do with us. He can help us to be shining lights in a dark world, holy children in an impure society. Spiritually we can be strong, beautiful, and influential in His cause of righteousness. We can be committed partners in our marriage. We can be dedicated parents instructing our children in the way of the Lord. We can set examples as employers, employees, and good neighbors. And get this – we can become effective in doing the Lord's specific work of bringing other souls to salvation, whether it is in the area of edification and building up or in primary obedience to the gospel of Christ's good news. God has never asked anyone to do anything they could not do, and he has asked all of the above of us. We need to listen to Him and have the confidence that He will stand with us. He says, "You can!"

We Can, Because Of Our Partnership

It is not because we are so wonderful and powerful that we are able to do these things. But listen to Paul's attitude in Philippians 4:13 when he says that he could do "all things through Christ who strengthens." This is the key to our power, our partnership with our heavenly Father and His Son. With them on our side we join the apostle in saying, "if God be for us who can be against us?" (Romans 8:31)

In Matthew 11:28-30 Jesus promises rest to those who are worn out with being battered by Satan and tired from life's burdens. Notice that He does not promise the burden bearing will stop. He simply says His burdens will be light and easy. There are two reasons for this.

First of all, it is simply easier on us to be followers of Christ than followers of Satan in most cases. The life of the child of God is more peaceful and gentler. His home is more loving and restful. His sleep is sound, and his conscience is clear without the worries that plague the wicked. In spite of what the modern media would report, the lives of the wicked are in turmoil. There is nothing "gay" about the homosexual lifestyle where a "committed" relationship is averaged out to be less than a month and the life span of a homosexual is on the average 20 years shorter than his heterosexual counterpart. Divorces seem to have leveled off over the last couple years, but perhaps this is because cohabitation without marriage is up. Single mother rates are skyrocketing. Child abuse rates are like juvenile crime rates, i.e., through the ceilings. While beer companies show us talking frogs, clear mountain streams, and bikini-clad girls, we're missing the real message of battered wives, highway deaths, unpaid bills, and the ever-increasing cost of insurance, law enforcement, medical expenses, and emotional tragedy. Teen suicide is the number two killer in our nation. Suing each other has become the national pastime. The best of our homes seem full of profane language, neglect of children, extra-marital affairs, and short on time for caring relationships. Does this sound like we're having a "good time" serving Satan? Sin is a tough master to be a slave to.

The second reason the yoke of Jesus is easy is simply because He shares it with us. That's the nature of a yoke; it is a shared burden. The man in the world is on his own. The man of God has a yoke fellow, a partner to share his burdens with. This co-worker we have has promised us He will never desert or forsake us, Hebrews 13:5. He is not a car salesman who is our best friend only as long as we're buying something from Him. He has shown His ability to love men by wishing forgiveness on those who nailed Him to the cross. We can confidently know there is nothing we can do that He will not forgive. With genuine repentance, we can always come home to Christ, and He will always share our load.

You want confidence? Listen to God. In 2 Timothy 1:7 the Spirit teaches that we are not created anew in Christ to be afraid and timid. God intends for us to recognize the spirit of power which He gives us. Paul prayed for

Christians to grow in this power which was and is available, Ephesians 3:14-16. In John 4:4 the apostle puts it in plain terms when he says the one who is in the child of God is greater than the one who is in the world. Christians have the edge; so, what is it we should fear? Be confident. You can grow up, mature in Christ, and serve Him faithfully.

What happens if we trip up? Well, John says the Scriptures are written so this would not happen, but what if it does? 1 John 4:4 reminds us that Jesus is still on our side. He is our advocate, 1 John 2:1. An "advocate" is one who speaks for another, a representative, a lawyer. Jesus is speaking for us. The Greek word translated here by "advocate" is the same word which is translated "comforter" in John 14:26 in the King James Version. In this verse Jesus was trying to build the confidence of His apostles as He was leaving. He knew they had a tremendous task ahead of them in taking the gospel into all the world, but He also knew they could handle this "mission impossible" with His help. They just needed to know they would not be alone. We must come to realize the same thing in our own hearts. We are not alone; He's on our side. He completely understands loneliness, betrayal, and rejection. He did know fear before He was killed. He understands what a broken heart feels like, and He wants you to know that He's still on your side. He sympathizes and listens to us, Hebrews 4:15-16. If we need wisdom, courage, strength, or anything else, He's there. Whatever the child of God needs to do God's will, Paul said He would supply, Philippians 4:19. The Spirit told the Ephesians that even "exceeding, abundantly, beyond all that we ask or think," God could do! (Ephesians 3:20) If we are growing, we should not stumble, 2 Peter 1:10-11, but if we do stumble, Christ Jesus is there to help us get up and get going again. Listen to Him and be confident in His salvation.

A Confident Christian

A spirit of confidence in our lives can quite literally change our lives. A study done several years ago of "successful" graduates from Harvard was quite revealing. In spite of a superior education, the poll found that 85% of those deemed to be "successful" in their chosen fields, credited their success to attitude while in only 15% of the cases was it due to aptitude. The psychologist, William James, said, "One can alter his life by altering his attitude." Our heavenly Father said, "As a man thinks within himself, so is he."

You can defeat the recurring sin in your life. You can be more outgoing, friendly, forgiving, patient, hospitable, generous, loving, and caring. You can bridle tongue or temper. We can grow up in all aspects, into Christ. God says we can and He expects us to if we are going to be known as His children. He will help and bless our efforts.

QUESTIONS ON CHAPTER THREE

1. What is the principle of human nature that God has placed within each of us which can give us needed encouragement and power?

2. Where does faith proceed from?

3. Where is one source (among many) we can get confidence from?

4. Where do we lose our confidence?

5. How does our spiritual "bully" roar at us?

6. What are three mistaken ideas, which the devil uses as "confidence killers?"

7. What does God tell us about Satan that should help us not to listen to him?

8. Where does the power to "do" really come from?

9. Where does God teach you the answer to the above question?

10. Two reasons why Jesus' yoke is easy and light are…

11. If we fail God, where is our confidence then?

12. What is an "advocate?"

13. How does having an advocate encourage you?

14. To what extent can God help us?

A FIERY SPIRIT — LESSON 4

The young bride slowly walks down the aisle toward her groom. She glances at faces she will not remember and smiles a happy smile she doesn't feel at the moment. When the music stops she thinks that surely all must notice her gasping for breath, and her nightmare is stumbling as she moves from her father's arm to that of the waiting young man. She has planned this moment for months (perhaps years). What is the problem?

A 65-year-old man studies the stock market page of the paper barely hearing his wife speak of their plans, "now that he's retired." A small child can't seem to stop talking and laughing on Christmas Eve, while his sixteen-year-old brother, out on his first date, says good-bye on the doorstep of a schoolmate. He leans in for his first kiss and wonders what a heart attack feels like. Parents tremble as their daughter obeys the gospel in baptism or their son says his first public prayer in worship. A black belt breaks a stack of concrete blocks, and a thousand football fans leap to their feet screaming, in unison. A fireman enters a burning building and a helicopter pilot drops his machine toward a smoke flare in a small clearing. From wedding chapel to jungle, all of the above have something in common. They are all affected by, influenced, and sometime overcome with...ZEAL.

This Is The Flavor Of Life

Zeal is defined as eagerness and ardent desire. Thayer defines it as excitement of mind or fervor of spirit. It is more than just an interest in something; it is active interest. It is mentioned in one form or another in the New American Standard Bible 37 times. Some synonyms of zeal are ardor, intensity, and passion. A very special synonym might best describe the use of the word which we are applying in this lesson. That synonym is enthusiasm. Our word enthusiasm comes from the Greek word "entheos." Entheos literally means "God in us." When the living God is living in us we are quite literally "enthusiastic." That is real zeal.

Consider life, if you will, without any enthusiasm. Would you like to live without ever being "eager," "intense," or "passionate"? Imagine life without any "excitement of mind" or "fervor" in one's spirit. Can you see why zeal would be called the flavor of life? And if that is true of life in general, what about our spiritual lives? Somebody has died for us. Natural laws as we understand them have been shoved aside to prove His words true. We have been given a glimpse into the next life, a life of unimaginable bliss or incomparable horror. And we have been given the choice of which way we will go. Doomed to go one way, divine love helps us to avoid a fate that is literally worse than death itself. Are we excited about it? Are we joyful and enthusiastic? Christians are much like criminals on death row who, instead of seeing a dark chair at the end of their last walk, suddenly see the door opening to reprieve and freedom. Do you think the criminal might be a little "passionate" about his situation?

> **Where do we most often hear accusations of coldness, ritualism, or a lack of love? AT CHURCH!**

Yet, where do we most often hear accusations of coldness, ritualism, or lack of love? Is it not at "church"? I'll grant you; many times the accusations are untrue. They are more a reflection of the accuser's heart than the accused. But sometimes, now, aren't we afraid those accusers are right? Consider this, you don't have to beg an artist or an author to work on their "creation." It's much more likely you'll have to beg them to take a breath. You don't have to take a month to sell tickets to the Super Bowl or the Indy 500. It's more likely that if you don't have tickets in advance, you won't be going. The fans of these events are excited. Likewise, something is wrong when Christians must be begged to attend, pleaded with to teach, cajoled into working, or tricked into giving. Where is our interest, our excitement, and our passion? In Matthew 5:13 Jesus spoke of God's people when they lose their "flavor." Their lives become tasteless. We can do better. Besides, who would want a tasteless existence? We must do better and I believe most of us want to.

Enthusiasm Is Not Necessarily Good

Zeal is a feeling, an emotion. As such it really is not right or wrong in itself. Whether zeal is good or bad is determined by what stirs it up and what it is aimed at. In Romans 10:2-3 Paul expresses his concern for the Jews because although they were zealous, their "excitement of mind" was not being guided by knowledge. They were "doing" without regard to God's concerns. As a result, they were "doing" wrong. Paul was truly the one to understand this in his Jewish brethren because in Philippians 3:6 he describes the same attitude in himself of being "enthusiastically wrong" as he persecuted the church. This shows us that we need to be careful of misguided zeal. Zeal, or enthusiasm, which is not directed properly, can cause one to…

Despise others we deem to be worse than ourselves. This was the problem with the scribes in Mark 2:14-16 who were very zealous for the letter of the law and very impatient with those who did not seem to be living according to their understanding.

Make unreasonable demands of others, like John in Mark 9:38. The demand from the apostle for the unnamed man to quit casting out demons because he was not in "John's crowd," made perfect sense to John. However, it would have made very little sense to one who was casting out evil spirits and effectively using the power of God already. John was not able to understand this, however, since his zeal had him focused in only on those who were "doing what he was doing" and "going where he was going."

Lose the sense of who we are as James and John did in Luke 9:51-56. Being extremely enthusiastic for their Lord, these two men considered the insult of the Samaritans here to be unacceptable in every way and behavior worthy of death. In their desire to defend the honor of their Lord they forgot that the business of Christ was to save men, not destroy them.

Have you ever been enthusiastic about something and attempted to get someone else interested? Have you ever been tempted to think a little less of someone who wasn't interested in your "product," or who couldn't seem to make the sacrifice of personal time or family time that you were willing to make? If you have, then you have tasted a little bit of what misguided zeal can do. The impatience which creeps into our actions and causes us to condemn and demand of others is not a pretty sight. It doesn't have to be this way, however. There is an "excitement" of mind, which is good, wholesome, and valuable to our spirit of growth.

A Fire In Our Bones

In Jeremiah's day Judah was in trouble. Jeremiah was called of God and committed to the cause of making the Jews see that in his lifetime the nation was going to be punished severely for turning away from God. His message was not a pleasant one, and he was not well received. It seems the confidence of the people was placed in the wise men and religious leaders of that day (18:18), men who were deceiving the people for hire. The only attention they gave Jeremiah was to "devise plans" to harm him and to "strike at him" with their tongues. The prophet was ignored, beaten, and put in stocks (20:2), and forbidden by God to have even the comfort of a wife and family (16:2). At times he was cursed (15:10), and once his life was threatened by the men of his own hometown (11:18-21). On other occasions men of influence and power threatened his life, and he was caused to suffer miserably from hunger and being left at the bottom of a well. At times the mocking and derision caused Jeremiah to desire to give in and stop speaking his important message. But 20:9 reveals another struggle the prophet had to face. He says the effort to contain the word of the Lord and not speak it anymore was like a "burning fire shut up in my bones." The effort of holding it in would tire him until he simply could not endure it. Jeremiah had to speak!

This "fire" of Jeremiah's was a beneficial zeal. It was a motivation that could not be cooled or soothed. Like a burn on his flesh, this ache in the prophet so obsessed him that it could not be ignored. Every Christian who desires to grow and walk with God should pray for this same consuming passion. It is this "fire" which will bring us through the doubts and trials of this life. When one voice whispers within us to quit, rest, or stop for just awhile, it is this "fervency of spirit" which will motivate us to act.

What Type Of "Fire" Should A Christian Have?

A Fire for knowledge and understanding of God's word. Before the New Testament scriptures were completed during the time God was providing miraculous spiritual gifts to teach His people, He was extremely concerned about these two things. In the list of miraculous gifts given in 1 Corinthians 12:8-10 are two specific teaching gifts, i.e., the word of wisdom and the word of knowledge. We can learn from our heavenly Father's interest here the importance of both of these. Certainly knowledge is important and especially knowledge of God's revelation to us. Without it we are like children in the dark without a lantern. If knowledge is a lantern (David called it a light to our path), however, wisdom is the match to light it. Wisdom makes it useful to us. James says that one who has the facts he needs but lacks the sense (wisdom) to put that information to use is deluded and ineffectual, James 1:22-26. Sadly, this word "ineffectual" describes the spiritual life of many and here is the reason why. While learning "the facts" we have failed to make the changes.

Every Christian absolutely needs a fire for the knowledge that is contained within God's word and an equal passion to see this knowledge put into practice. Peter calls this fire a longing in 1 Peter 2:2. If we're going to grow up in Christ, we need an enthusiasm for the "pure milk of the word" that is comparable to the enthusiasm a newborn baby has for mother's breast. In other words, we must have it in regular, satisfying feedings. The apostle says this will help us grow with respect to salvation.

A Fire for the needs of others. The urgent interest of the church in Achaia for the welfare of poor saints at Jerusalem not only led them to spend a year gathering funds together to send (2 Corinthians 8:10), it also stirred up the churches in Macedonia to become interested and involved in this work, 2 Corinthians 9:2. To dedicate such a period of time to fundraising and saving money is in itself a tremendous accomplishment for that early congregation. What makes this a splendid example of the power of zeal, however, is realizing that all the funds and all this effort were for people who the Corinthians had probably never even met. It was for Jewish Christians (a race of people who could hardly be well known for their patience and benevolence in dealing with Gentiles). Their passion for the need, however, as well as for doing right (2 Corinthians 7:11) led them to immerse themselves in this mighty effort of international benevolence, overcome all stumbling blocks the devil could have used, and succeed at their work.

In this Gentile effort we see the same love and concern for brethren that we witnessed at the beginning of the church when Christians who had extra land or houses sold them so the benevolent needs of their brethren could be seen to. We need this same concern.

A Fire for the salvation of others. Our Lord's passion for the salvation of men was so great that he lost His appetite at the prospect of reaching others with His Father's message, John 4:8, 31-34. The apostles were willing to accept threats, imprisonment, and beatings in order to continue speaking, Acts 4:21; 5:40-42. This fervor of spirit in the early Christians was so great that when civil and religious leaders began putting pressure on them, they immediately prayed for more confidence and boldness to keep speaking the name of Jesus, Acts 4:29-31. These folks were "fired up." They had a grasp of the blessings, which were being offered, and the price to be paid for sin and they simply were not content to let others fall into Satan's traps without a fight.

Just while you have been reading this lesson, hundreds have left this world unprepared for judgment. Can any child of God not be impassioned by that fact.

A Fire for commitment to moral values. In a society, which more and more is commending evil and demeaning good, one will have to be "fired up" to avoid confusion and temptation. We need the "active interest" to speak of and practice sexual purity, to hold fast this teaching with the next generation while the world says, "you can't say no." We need a strong passion for our families as the world drives its wedges in and seeks to tear them apart. We need the strength of an iron commitment to the fact that lying is wrong... ALWAYS. Cheating, stealing (even a little), and slander are sinful. We need to be so committed to God's moral value system that we can accept the fact that our hearts need the purifying influence of His Spirit and that we need to say, "No," to much of what is called entertainment today.

Nobody is forcing us to buy CDs and tapes that encourage evil activity, go to movies which graphically glorify sinful conduct, or invite such into our homes via TV. We need to be praying for some of the same fire in our hearts that burned evil books in Acts 19:18-19 and eliminated their sinful practices with its heat.

A Fire for the acceptance of our responsibility. The Christian needs a fire burning so hot in his heart that excuses, rationalizations, and unjust comparisons to others just will not be able to stand the heat. Each of us needs to quit waiting on others to lead the way and start leading the way ourselves. We must quit applying the Scriptures to others and become like young Samuel, i.e., hearing God call us personally. Instead of answering, "Speak

Lord," too often we begin with "I can't," and no one will dare contradict us because they have their own "I cant's" to deal with.

If I will grow, then I must go! We must all realize the feeling that we have served too much, worked too hard, or been burdened unjustly are not feelings from God, but temptations from Satan. The weight lifter hears those same voices also telling him, "That's enough weight for today." He knows he cannot listen, however, and succeed. He can't stop lifting and also keep his muscles growing. Christians must learn this lesson also. Quite waiting. Pray for a fire that will make it too hot for us to stop and sit still.

A Fire for God's House. Isaiah 59:17 describes God in similar fashion to the Christian soldier in Ephesians 6. After the description of His armor, however, the prophet describes God as being wrapped up in a mantle of zeal. What a beautiful picture of terrible passion, our God bringing vengeance on His enemies as a well armored soldier going into battle wrapped about with fervent enthusiasm. This "active interest" was not lost on His Son as the prophets declared that one of Jesus' characteristics was He would be "consumed" with zeal for God's house. This passion is illustrated in John 2:13-17. Christ is our example, 1 Peter 2:21. God's house today is the church, the kingdom, 1 Peter 2:5.

We desperately need this fire our Lord had. We need a hot zeal for every aspect of the church. Some have tried to insert excitement into worship as a substitute for zeal for His church. This has been tried with singing groups, instrumental music, drama productions, etc. The excitement produced by these things is a temporary heat, however, having more foundation in variety than spirituality. We must grow to the point of realizing there is no new gospel, no new church, no new worship which will make us zealous. We must learn to rekindle our passion in the available power of God that we overlook so often. We can get enthusiastic about the spiritual work given to us, the uniqueness of who we are in this world, and the wonderful providence of a God who cares about us as individuals.

We Need Motivation

A few years ago outside Dallas, Texas a truck wrecked and rolled off the highway. Passing motorists attempted to help the driver who was crushed between the roof and steering wheel while his feet were pinned between the pedals of the brake and clutch. Jacks and chains were seemingly useless in getting the truck door open, though several were struggling to help him. Suddenly someone in the gathering crowd shouted, "Fire!" as smoke puffed from under the hood and at the same time filled the passenger compartment. As the would-be rescuers backed away from the truck a lone black man ran from the crowd. By himself, he wrenched the door off the wrecked vehicle, wriggled into the cab and using his back, pushed the roof up to free the man. Witnesses said that he beat the flames in the floorboard out with his hands before he single-handedly pulled the pedals apart to free the man's foot and then carried him to safety before disappearing back into the crowd. He remains a nameless rescuer to this day. What magnificent efforts come forth when we are just "motivated" to action.

Zealous motivation is what Christ desires of us. He wants us on fire to do good for Him because people are trapped and perishing, Titus 2:4. He wants us "deeply concerned" over our brethren, Colossians 4:13. Our Lord knows that enthusiasm is catching, 2 Corinthians 9:2. It's hard not to be motivated to be more active in service. We assist our brethren to be this way and fulfill other commands to stimulate and encourage them, Hebrews 10:24. We grow and mature and in so doing, we help others to do likewise.

Things Which Encourage Enthusiasm

Just think about some things which get you excited. What really interests you? What gets you dreaming? What things do you get enthused about? The same aspects of the things, which interest you, will also help your interest in spiritual things. Think of each of the following as a single match. One is plenty if it catches fire correctly, but just in case it doesn't, the more the merrier. A few of the things, which can help us to be more zealous, are…

Variety. Little changes, new perspectives, personal touches, as in a marriage for example, can renew enthusiasm. Some make the mistake of seeking new mates when just small changes can be exciting. Changes in worship, methods, etc. can add to a fervent spirit.

Investment. Just like the stock market, when we invest $500 or $5000, that page of the paper suddenly takes on greater importance. When we invest more time, money, or effort in our spiritual lives, they suddenly begin to mean more to us.

Success. Positive feedback is always exciting. It may be a type of reward motivation, but it works well. It means setting some reachable goals or participating in an effort where results are going to be good. This will encourage you to try more lofty challenges and seek victories there also.

Love. Focusing on love, doing what's best for the other person is a tremendous motivator. Just ask any mother. When we love God we will follow all His commandments, 1 John 5:3. When we slow down and learn to love people we will be motivated to help, teach, rebuke, exhort, whatever is necessary.

Others. Enthusiasm is contagious. We can catch it or we can pass it on. If you want it, schedule time in your life to be around people who are that way. Question them, listen to them, and absorb their positive outlook. If you want to see more of it, develop it within yourself – others will catch it from you. Plan group activities and participate in them.

Satisfaction. There is a feeling of accomplishment and pride that comes with completing a task well. Every house builder and wall painter knows the feeling. If you get a taste of it in spiritual efforts, you will never be the same. Every man or woman who has ever taken the gospel into a foreign field or met a stranger and led them to know Christ, has tasted the contentment and peace that is the reward for such labor. It is a contentment that is hard to rest with because there is always the desire for more.

Loyalty. Like love, this is a powerful force to build enthusiasm. Most screaming alumnus in the football stadiums of their favorite schools know this feeling. The soldier on a dangerous mission for his country knows this feeling. It is sad, but in both these cases sometimes more loyalty is shown than by the Christian who owes so much to his Lord. As we meditate on our own unworthiness and the relationship of love Jesus desires to have with us, feelings of debt and loyalty can grow into strong motivators.

Fun. Most people are excited by things which are distracting, entertaining, or recreational (re-creating self?). Spiritual things can also be fun, however. They don't have to be silly, and thoughts of sin, punishment, death, and salvation are certainly not humorous. But there should be a good spirit of enjoyment in much of our association with one another. With all the rejoicing

Christians ought to have in their lives, wouldn't it be strange if children of God acted as if they could not laugh?

Conclusion

With all of the preceding factors helping us to be excited in mind, fervent in spirit, interested and passionate about who we are and what we are doing, there's simply no excuse for failing to be zealous.

Jesus wants you this way,
others need you this way,
you need to be this way to grow,
and you will just enjoy life more.

Zeal is the flavor of life and Christians cannot afford to become tasteless.

QUESTIONS ON LESSON FOUR

1. How would you define zeal?

2. What synonym best brings the idea of spiritual zeal across? Why?

3. What are some reasons that come to your mind as to why zeal may be lacking in some congregations?

4. Why does zeal need to be considered and directed?

...Growth in New Testament churches   *page 39*

5. Are there any negative aspects to Jeremiah's zeal that you can think of?

6. In your mind, what types of changes might come about in churches if more people suddenly developed the "fire in the bones" type zeal of Jeremiah?

7. List 6 types of zeal every Christian should have (an easy question).

8. List any other types of "fire" you feel Christians should "set" (a hard question).

9. How do you think one might develop more zeal for God's house without changing any scriptural admonition on the church's work and/or worship?

10. In your mind, and by your definition...How important is "motivation"?

11. Take 3 things from the list of "Things which encourage enthusiasm," apply them to the individual Christian or the congregation, and make an application of how enthusiasm/zeal might be encouraged.

LESSON 5   A PRAYERFUL SPIRIT

The Indianapolis star ran a report given out over Israeli radio in January of 1993. It seems the National Telephone Company of Israel, Bezek, was publicizing a new phone number in Jerusalem to which believers could send their prayers via FAX machine. A Bezek employee would then take a copy of the prayer and stuff it into a crevice in the "Wailing Wall," the only part of the Jewish temple still standing. According to tradition, prayers poked in between the wall's rough stone blocks are likely to be answered in the affirmative by God. The end of the article, however, stated that the Bezek service was not guaranteeing a reply.

It seems the 20th century man's need for prayer and the hope of an affirmative answer has finally met technology. I will let you judge as to whether faxed prayers on paper inserted into old walls carries more attention getting power with God than sincere supplication from obedient hearts. But, the fact remains in the account above, there would not have been such a service offered if there was not a strong desire for communication with God.

Increasingly More Commonplace

W. M. Linz, President of Crossroads, a major publisher of serious religious books, says, "After the Bible, books on prayer are our biggest sellers." The 1992 edition of Books in Print listed nearly 2,000 titles on prayer, meditation, and techniques for spiritual growth – that's more than three times the number devoted to sexual intimacy and how to achieve it. The old advertising slogan of "sex sells…" may not be as true as most of us are led to believe when it is really placed alongside of the spiritual needs of men and women. An article in Newsweek magazine points out that in America, as the prophet Amos put it, these types of conversations (prayers) "flow like a mighty river." If you believe in opinion surveys, more Americans this week

will pray than will go to work, or exercise, or have sexual relations. Seventy-eight percent of Americans report praying once a week, 57% once a day, and even among the 13% of Americans which claim to be atheists or agnostics, nearly one in five still prays daily (betting that there is a God who hears them?) **A Poloma and Gallup Poll says...**
- 91% of women pray, as do 85% of men
- 94% of blacks pray, and 87% of whites
- 42% ask for material things when they pray
- 15% regularly receive a definite answer to specific prayer
- 27% never have received definite answers
- 25% have received definite answers once or twice
- 45% of 18-24 year olds pray meditatively
- 70% of 65 year olds pray meditatively

Since this study is mainly concerned with spiritual growth, we might add here that in addition to the obvious need for communication with God pointedly illustrated in the preceding figures, one simply cannot grow properly without it. What is prayer to the child of God?

Trying To Define It

Prayer is communication. It is dialog, conversation, praise, thanks, acknowledgment, intercession, supplication, and request. We could make it more mysterious by defining different Greek words which are used to represent prayer to us, but basically it is just communication with God. Although public praying should not be minimized, it is a serious work of leading other minds and spirits before God; our study deals mainly with private prayers. When it comes to growth, this is an area that cannot be overemphasized. The very synonyms at the beginning of this section should illustrate to our minds part of the reason why this subject is important. Imagine a child/father relationship without dialog, acknowledgment, request, etc. What a cold emotionless home that would be. As we learned in lesson three, however, our God is a God of passion who desires enthusiasm and zeal in His children. A relationship with God demands prayer because it demands communication.

Misunderstandings About Prayer

It's been said that anything which is generally understood is generally understood wrong. Not many areas of spirituality can claim to be more widely misunderstood and thus misapplied than the area of prayer. As we enter this study it is good for us to cleanse certain notions from our minds. Prayer is not…

A fire escape that is uncared for and unused except in case of emergencies.

A woodshed that we use to verbally (and sometimes publicly) punish people. A good example of this would be the well meaning brother serving communion one Lords' day evening who prayed, "Lord, we pray that those who are about to partake will think seriously about why they were not here this morning and that they will start being here so we will not have to do this every Sunday night."

A record or CD that is recorded word for word and then used for the pleasant sounds even though it has no life.

A bellhop's bell so we can tell God what to do with the baggage we're carrying around.

A substitute player to take the place of other responsibilities such as face-to-face apologies or rebukes.

An Aladdin's lamp that we can use to get whatever our heart wishes.

I grew up in North Alabama. In the congregations I attended it was quite common to see men kneeling in prayer. Some churches even had extra room between the pews just so the men could go to their knees. For a while, in my youth, I think I had the impression that this was the way preachers were supposed to pray, but I wasn't the only one. I recall an account of a brother about to lead a public prayer before an assembled student body at a Christian college. He had on the stage with him two more preaching brethren, one of whom was quite large of girth. Because of his doubts about the physical ability of the large brother to kneel, he simply stated that all would remain seated for prayer. Wherein, he was interrupted in his efforts and corrected by the third brother, who stated words to the effect that if brother _____ could not kneel, that was his problem, but as for the rest, they would be kneeling in prayer!

Obviously, many have felt the closer one got to the floor, the more effective his prayers were. Coming from a background like this you can imagine my feeling in moving to the north and worshipping with several congregations that seemed to think standing was the way to show respect in prayer. It makes sense doesn't it? After all, we stand to pledge the flag, and we stand in grand ovations to performers. Why should God get any less show of honor and respect?

The truth is, from God's heavenly perspective, posture is unimportant. Scriptural examples show us wonderful men of faith who prayed as they stood looking up, kneeling, or fell on their faces prostrate on the ground. Nehemiah 2:4 records for us how Nehemiah prayed to God when he was asked a question by the Persian King, Artaxerxes, whom he was serving. Did he kneel down or close his eyes and speak to himself? The king would have thought him mad. No, the truth is he communicated with God for the briefest of moments as he recognized himself suddenly with opportunity and great need. He would not have done this if he had not already been of the attitude of constant regular prayer, as Christians are later told to do. Whether praying all night to our Lord, in a brief thought like Nehemiah, or somewhere in between, our heavenly Father desires communication with His children. Standing, sitting, kneeling, or prostrate, He wants communication.

Why Is Prayer A Blessing?

We sing about the blessing in prayer and we speak about it, but exactly why is prayer a blessing?

Partially because it is a privilege to be able to be like Christ. The apostles were so impressed with the prayer life of the Master they requested to be taught how to pray. We fall so far short of being like Jesus in so many things, it is a blessing to be given something like prayer which we can develop and grow in so as to be more like Him as time goes on.

It is a blessing because it is an effective way to fight Satan. When our Lord spoke to believers about the coming destruction of Jerusalem in Luke 21, one of the last admonitions was in verse 36, an admonition to use prayer faithfully so they might have strength to overcome what was coming. I wonder how many stumbling blocks we would dodge if we prayed daily about avoiding temptations like Jesus taught in Matthew 6:13. In James 4:7 the Spirit says to resist Satan and he will flee. The logic of this is seen in the fact that it is difficult to spend devoted, sincere time in prayer about a temptation – and then go give in. It's said Satan trembles when the weakest saints get on their knees.

Although not intended to be used selfishly, prayer is a way to get our requests from God. James said, "You do not receive, because you do not ask." Maybe the slip of the tongue of one song leader bringing a worship to an end is closer to the truth than we want to admit. That song leader announced the end of the service by announcing, "Brother _____ will now close our minds in prayer." Have we closed our minds to the fact that our God answers prayer? Read again Matthew 7:7-11 and ask yourself if your heavenly Father can at least match up with earthly fathers who grant good requests of their children.

Prayer is a means of fellowship. Isn't it interesting how the Scriptures teach us that God knows what we need before we ask (Matthew 6:32), but He still wants us to ask, Luke 18:1.

I left for college in late August. One Sunday morning before Thanksgiving someone banging on my door awakened me. There was a phone call. My father's voice was the first thing I heard when I answered the phone, so I immediately guessed there must be something wrong. There was, and it was me. He had waited patiently as long as he could, but after receiving a letter from the Dean of Students it seemed he thought he should call. He wanted to make sure the student named in the letter was his son. He couldn't be sure, because although he had sent his son to that school, he had not heard a word since, not in three months. I got the message. My parents wanted to hear from me.

And your heavenly Father wants to hear from you. He wants the relationship of communication and caring. He wants the sharing (i.e., fellowship) of your life, your spiritual tumbles, and your growth.

Prayer brings peace. In the 60's Harvard Cardiologist Herbert Benson discovered practitioners of meditation could reduce stress by sitting quietly and repeating a mantra. He found that almost any uttered soothing sound would produce the same physiological response. Further experiments have turned up even more information. Dr. Benson has noticed patients who prayed were even more successful at lowering metabolic rates and controlling symptoms of stress than those who used religiously insignificant words to calm their minds. "Dr." Paul said it a little differently in Philippians 4:6, but read this passage and see if he's not teaching peace is a promise from God for the praying Christian.

Prayer is a blessing because when we focus our minds and hearts we often cannot help but get up off our knees wanting to work. This spiritual focus, if engaged in on a regular basis, can change us, and when we change then things around us change also. We just won't let them rest.

Prayer Should Be Easy

Prayer is communication, right? Everybody communicates so everybody ought to be able to master prayer, wrong. One of the closest and most intimate relationships of life is marriage. If any two people ought to be able to communicate it ought to be a husband and wife. Yet, we are told over and over that one of the main problems in marriages is a lack of communication. People live with one another for decades and never learn to speak their real feelings or truly hear what their spouse may be saying. They never really learn to communicate. My point is that even in this life, when we can see another person face to face, communication takes some effort. Can it require any less effort when we communicate with the God of heaven and earth? But, just like in our marriage, it is worth it?

Consider also how our loving Father has tried to make it as easy as possible. He has given us a mediator, a go-between who knows both sides, frail humanity as well as omnipotent deity, 1 Timothy 2:5. This High Priest, Jesus Christ, is a sympathetic mediator who is full of mercy and favor toward us, Hebrews 4:15-16. It's a little like having a mediator in a labor dispute down at the local factory who favors the side of the workers and is willing to make up any lack on their part out of his own pocket. Even when we sin we are encouraged not to give up because He will never quit on us. He continues to speak for us with the Father seeking forgiveness for all those who keep trying to do their very best, Hebrews 13:5-6; 1 John 1:7; 2:1.

God also considers this form of communication so important that special help in this area has been granted. The apostle Paul, after many years of Spirit filled service, makes a surprising statement in Romans 8:26 when he says, "We do not know how to pray as we should..." Well, if Paul didn't know, how can I? The truth is, it doesn't matter. You and I have the same help in our prayers as Paul did. God has given His Spirit to "intercede" or go on behalf of another. The same one who searches the thoughts of God (1 Corinthians 2:11) searches your thoughts also. He can present our petitions to the Father even when we feel "the words just won't come." His efforts on our behalf are even beyond the expression of words. The Christian does not have to fear that any of his prayers will fall short because he has two helpers who are ready and willing and able to lift his petitions up before God while these helpers interpret, emphasize and take the side of God's child.

But, What About My Part?

Communication cannot be just one sided. Truly, there are aspects of our lives which we must tend to in order to make acceptable supplication to our God. For example, one who prays needs to have an attitude of...

Selflessness. By this I mean the Christian should have a sense of spirituality about his prayer, rather than carnality. Whether it is how he prays or for what he prays there should be an understanding of the importance of this dialog with the creator and the relative unimportance of other things such as pride, worldly desires, etc., Matthew 6:5-6; James 4:3.

Sincerity. Men often have chosen written words for prayers rather than trusting God's word that His desire was for heart-felt expression. This is not to say writing a prayer down nullifies its effect, but there is always the danger of repeating words for their attractive sound rather than focusing on the act of communicating with our God. The Father's primary interest is in sincere expression of ones inner being, Matthew 6:7; John 4:24.

Penitence. The blessing of prayer is a blessing that has always been available to children of the living God and unavailable to those who reject Him. It is a relationship blessing, a right of birth. Those not in the family have never had the promise of this access to the Father. This is a difficult concept to grasp in our modern, enlightened age of broad-minded tolerance, but this is truth nonetheless. God has given His word on prayer to His children, those who strive to defeat sin and follow His directions, 1 Peter 3:12; Proverbs 28:9;

Psalms 66:18.

Understanding. This concept is tied closely to the previously mentioned "sincerity." One needs to understand what he is praying for or about. We lack understanding when we read or memorize prayers, repeating them without thought. We also lack understanding when we imitate the prayers of others without thinking of what is being said and we use vocabulary that is beyond our knowledge. Do we think God is impressed with our "word power?" 1 Corinthians 14:15

> (Side note: Some real examples of people praying "without understanding" what they are saying would be the men who prayed the following prayers...
> - In the worship assembly you might often have heard prayers "for all those who are sick of this congregation."
> - Or requests made to, "keep us free from the molestation of men." (A good prayer for the sisters in some congregations, I'm sure)
> - But pity the brother who said at the Lord's Table, "we ask your blessing on this fruit of the loom,"
> - Or in another prayer, "please forgive us our falling shorts."
>
> -We need to pray with understanding!)

Forgiveness. Our Lord focused strongly on the idea of mistakenly expecting from God what we are not willing to give ourselves. The one who holds grudges should not be surprised if God does the same. And who has more right? This important life principle is incorporated by Christ into our prayer life in Matthew 6:12-15.

Cooperation. This last mentioned aspect has to do with a principle of revelation. God reveals His will because He expects us to follow it. Our God expects us to act. When Jesus told 12 men He would make them "fishers of men," He expected them to follow. When He gave the Great Commission, He expected them to go! When He gave Peter permission to walk on the water, He expected him to get out of the boat and walk. The attitude we see in the religious world today of "salvation is by faith, not works, therefore I don't have to do anything" is nothing short of blasphemy. Many people have allowed themselves to be convinced it doesn't matter what they do, how they talk, where they worship, or when and if they worship at all. The Christian understands that He is a "servant," like his Lord. God expects us to "do"! Prayer is wonderful, but God also expects us to act upon our prayer. Pray for the lost, the sick, and the weak –and then get busy. Pray with faith for the mountain to be moved, then get up and get your shovel.

When one is praying in faith and sincerity while diligently trying to forgive others, when he is praying with a selfless attitude and penitent heart which is trying to know God's will and do it, and when he is praying with the intent of serving God and putting his hand to God's work, then he is praying "according to God's will" (1 John 5:14-15) and is promised an answer.

How Much Does Prayer Mean To You?

How important is communication to a plane trying to land in a thick fog, or a ship trying to make its way through reefs and shoals? How important is communication to help guide a child through the pitfalls of adolescence into adulthood? Each of these in its own way represents the Christian making his way past spiritual obstacles toward spiritual goals.

The apostles thought prayer such an important part of serving Christ that they would not sacrifice it to physically serve others. They found other ways to make sure widows were cared for as they kept their priority in serving their Lord, Acts 6:4. We cannot allow prayer to be pushed out of our daily lives either by the many requirements placed upon us by others or by our own conscience desiring to do more to help others. Prayer must be a priority.

When Should We Pray?

Daniel prayed three times daily and would give it up for no one, including the king himself, even if it meant losing his own life. David prayed "morning by morning" and Jesus arose "a great while before day," Psalms 5:3; Mark 13:5. Paul said to do it without ceasing and at all times, while Jesus taught His disciples to do it always, 1 Thessalonians 5:17; Ephesians 6:18; Luke 18:2. Obviously, prayer is something which ought to be a daily aspect of life as a child of God. Communicating with our heavenly Father is a "must," a necessity, and if done in the proper spirit and with an obedient life, it promises great peace and spiritual help on our road toward full growth.

My prayer will be with you as you study these lessons and seek to grow more like your Lord.

In Conclusion

Several good suggestions for developing a meaningful prayer life might be in order here. Like most things of worth, this too does not happen by accident, it takes thought and organization.

Have a prayer list. It's easy for most of us to forget things if we don't write them down. Jot down people (by name) and situations, which you feel, need prayer. And keep it updated - you will be surprised at how long this list will become and how many answers you will see God give.

Organize your list. As the list grows you may want to dedicate different days to different subjects in addition to daily general prayers. Just for example, one church bulletin I saw encouraged people to line up subjects that began with the same letter of the day they were prayed for, as follows…

Sunday – pray for saints and sinners

Monday – missionaries and money (to do God's work)

Tuesday – teachers, trials, and temptations

Wednesday – Washington (our gov't) and "Whys" (questions you have)

Thursday – Thanksgiving and thoughtfulness (deed done by others)

Friday – Family (every part of it)

Saturday – Shut-ins, sick, suffering (mournful)

Develop good prayer habits. Set aside time to pray daily and be open for other times, which may be provided. Several years ago I was acquainted with a good sister who started getting up a few minutes early every morning in order to begin her day's priorities with her prayer list. The only way I found out about it was that she commented one day how many of her prayers were being answered and how it had helped her attitude. I immediately requested to be put on her list!

One last point of interest. We can study prayer, define prayer, and pick apart all the different aspects of developing a faithful prayer life until we reduce it to its most antiseptic properties. When all things are considered, however, most all can pray meaningful prayers when we understand our need and truly believe that answers can be forthcoming. Toward the goal of motivated prayer we dedicate the following.

The Best Way

Some say down on your knees,
is the proper way to pray.
Others stand up straight,
say that's the better way.
Some pray while seated
and simply bow their heads.
Others prefer to lie face down,
prone upon their beds.
Some pray out in the sunshine
with tightly closed eyes.
While others like the darkness
and gaze toward the sky.
This winter in the shopping center,
I lost my balance twice,
The best prayers I ever prayed,
I was sprawled out on the ice!

THOUGHT QUESTIONS ON LESSON FIVE

1. Why might one think man has an inner need to communicate with God?

2. Define prayer in your own words.

3. Name three misunderstandings that people sometimes have about prayer.

...Growth in New Testament churches   *page 51*

4. What is the scriptural posture for engaging in prayer?

5. Name 5 reasons why we might refer to prayer as a blessing

6. Can you name any more reasons why prayer might be a blessing to you?

7. How has our heavenly Father sought to make prayer as easy as possible?

8. What are some things that will help our petitions to be acceptable to God?

9. Turn your answers to number 8 around and name some things that will make our prayers unacceptable.

10. What are some things we can do to help us develop and mature in our prayer life? (Feel free to use the suggestions in the lesson, but add to them if you can.)

LESSON 6   A COMMITTED SPIRIT

Read the headlines any week of the year. Why does it seem that 100 million church members have less impact than the one percent of our population who claim to be homosexual? Which group is getting protective laws passed on state as well as federal levels? Which group does Hollywood and society, in general, hesitate to mock? It has not always been this way.

Drive down the "church row" in your town and look at the meeting times that are listed on the signs in front of the different church buildings. Several years ago most of them would have been scheduling morning and evening services. Today, most have changed over to some sort of recreation for the young people on Sunday night or cancelled services altogether. What is going on?

What's happening is that, as always, the attitudes of people are being reflected in their lifestyles. And it is not just happening at church on Sunday evening or in Washington. Look at the problems we are facing in this country, in our homes, and marriages. America has one of the highest divorce rates in the world. About fifty percent of all marriages are either on the rocks or headed for them. This is in addition to the fact that more people are living together without bothering to marry than ever before. They live with the knowledge that if times get tough they can just move out and find another partner. And if we can believe the surveys which are being answered by many of our friends and neighbors, well over half of all husbands and wives are cheating on their spouses. Over a decade ago we began hearing about the problems of "latch-key" kids. These are children who come home to an empty house and no adult supervision because both mom and dad are working. Almost every week, it seems, we hear of another newborn child somewhere who has been discovered in a trash can or back alleyway, abandoned. And then there's that small, but vocal, hard-core group of individuals in our society which advocates killing a child in the womb if it is inconvenient for the mother to have a child. All of these terrible attitudes and problems are tied together with a common string, i.e., a lack of commitment!

In the interest of immediate gratification many are laying aside their commitment to their spouse, their children, their God, their church, their country, and even the self-respect which comes from taking responsibility for their own actions. A lack of commitment is one of the greatest problems the Christian will have to face as he struggles to grow up in Christ and bear fruit. It simply has become too acceptable to fade out, give up, or quit.

What Are We Speaking Of?

There are at least ten different Greek words, which are translated by various forms of the word "commitment." One of these is found in 1 Peter 4:19 where Christians who are suffering righteously are encouraged to "entrust" their souls to a faithful Creator. The word paratithemi literally means to lay down. The picture is one of God's children laying down their souls or spirits at the feet of their Creator for care since their bodies were being handed over to the enemy for suffering and even for death. They were "committed" to their cause, "committed" to their Savior, and they showed it by "entrusting" their most precious possession, i.e., their soul, to Him for safekeeping. It is much the same thought as the first prayer many children learn. Now I lay me down to sleep, I pray the Lord my soul to keep. Peter, by the Spirit, was encouraging those Christians to commit themselves to God and trust Him to preserve their spirits safe from harm or loss.

Another form of the term commitment is found in John 2:24. In this passage Jesus is preaching in Jerusalem, but the Scriptures tell us that He was, to some extent, withholding Himself from the people. He knew the possibilities for harm that dwelt within the very ones who were listening to Him. He understood the fickle nature of men and how they are able to change from adoration to hatred in just a short time. Knowing the heart of man, as the passage tells us He did, as well as the work, which He still had before Him, Jesus could not take the chance in completely trusting all those who followed Him. The New American Standard Bible reads that He was "not entrusting Himself to them." In other words, He was not laying himself open completely to these people, trusting in them, having faith in them. His commitment to their salvation was complete, but His handing of Himself over to them fully was to come later. He was holding back.

Commitment is more than just believing in something or trusting someone. It is the actual handing over of self to that which we are committed. It is believing enough in something or someone that we will lay down self at their feet for them to do as they wish. John 12:48 records for us the account of many Jewish rulers who were believing in Jesus. Although the Scriptures plainly show they were believers, they were not committed. They did not trust in His messiahship to the extent that they could lay down their pride and confess Him. They were still protecting themselves. When we are committed, self-protection is the least of our concerns.

Commitment To A Person Is The Point Of No Return

While living out west a few years ago, I worked with the Sheriffs Department as part of their Rescue and Recovery dive unit. It was sad work when we were called out to search for drowning victims, but it was also interesting when we were diving for stolen property, evidence in criminal cases, and experimenting with new diving equipment. A good part of our work was done in the Missouri River where special care had to be exercised. The Missouri, where it runs between Iowa and Nebraska, has been channeled and wingdiked by the Corp of Engineers until it runs with a dangerously strong current for underwater work. To work in the river one was required to strap on about one hundred and fifty pounds of lead. There is no visibility, so everything has to be done by touch. There is the constant danger of getting one's air and radio lines tangled in stumps, fence posts, barbwire, and anything else that people have thrown into the water upstream for almost a hundred miles. After a couple of "interesting" incidents with the crew which manned the safety lines and air hose, including having to walk out of the current myself because my lines were fouled on a stump and the crew had "lost" me, I remember being greatly relieved when a personal friend of mine joined the unit. Why was I relieved? It was because when I was in some barbwire with no visibility in an eight-knot current, I could be sure that there was someone on the other end of that rope who was committed to me. Would you rather have your life in the hands of someone who had made a "decision" to be there, or someone who had a commitment to you?

This is exactly the same problem many Christians and many congregations have. They had made a decision, but they are not committed to a person. It is this personal commitment to an individual that is needed. Jesus desires us to be committed to Him. Decisions are fine, but they can change, and often are changed when the situation changes. It is not the decision to marry, but the commitment to a person, that made Philip Bliss go back into a burning train car to try and save the life of his wife, losing his own in the process. It is not the decision to join the army, but the commitment to a person, that causes one man to risk his life for his friend on the battlefield. It is not the decision to have children, but the commitment to a son or daughter, that makes parents run back into burning buildings. I repeat, Jesus desires a personal commitment to Him. It is not the decision to obey the gospel that will make us grow and help us to be steadfast through the years; it is the commitment to the person, to our Savior and friend, Jesus.

Think for a moment, this may be a scary question. Have you "committed" yourself to Jesus Christ? I mean without reservation, holding back, hesitation, or bargaining? Have you laid down yourself at His feet to be available in whatever way He could use you, or have you said, "no" from time to time? "I'll do this for you, Lord," we might say, "But I think you should ask someone else to do the other." If you have not fully trusted Him to do right and care for you, even though you could not see the end of the matter, then you aren't committed. There's no such thing as partial commitment! Now, please understand me. I'm not speaking of different levels of commitment. Of course, there are different levels. That is why the Spirit speaks of the babe in Christ as well as the mature one. When one obeys the gospel as a youth, it certainly is not possible to have the level of commitment of one who has been studying and practicing godliness for fifty or sixty years. It is not even possible to have the maturity of one who has been serving Christ for half that long. However, on whatever level of growth we find ourselves, it is certainly is possible to be fully and completely committed to our Lord. In this way I say there is no partial commitment. It is either all or nothing.

When a plane moves down the runway there is a point of no return for the pilot. As the plane picks up speed, the pilot must decide whether to take off or abort the take-off. Once he passes the point of no return, he is committed. If he changes his mind, it is too late, the plane will crash. When one decides to come to the Lord in obedient baptism he is getting on the plane and starting the engines. There is going to come a time, however, when the pre-flight check and warm-up is over. If we are going to grow and bear fruit we must commit to the man Jesus. We must trust Him and take off. Too many Christians and too many churches sit on the runway and gun their engines and then throttle down at the point of no return. Rather than leap into the sky full of power and off on a mission, they put on the brakes and go back to the hanger for a while. What a waste.

The Call To Commitment

Romans 12:1-2 presents the Christian's call to commitment. The Spirit there, through the writing of the apostle Paul, "urges us by the mercies of God" to "present our bodies" as a living and holy "sacrifice."

By our "bodies," he does not mean our hands and feet (although these would be included). He is speaking of our hearts, our attitudes, our loves, our spirit, and our very lives. We are urged by the Spirit of God to give everything up to God, lay these things down at His feet and trust Him to use them to glorify Himself and make us fruitful. This means no sign posting on different parts of our lives. Whether it is our friendships, our families, our job, our schooling, or our recreations – no posting signs! You know the ones I mean. We must tear down the signs in our lives that say, KEEP OUT, or NO TRESPASSING, PRIVATE, or RESERVED. It is all or nothing with our Lord. Nathaniel is a good example of this trait. Jesus commended him, when He said, "Behold, an Israelite in whom is no guile." To have no guile is to be transparent, to have nothing hidden, no deceit, no hidden motives. This is the way that our lives should be.

The word Paul uses, "present," is the technical word for "offer a sacrifice." It literally meant to relinquish, yield, or make a presentation. God wants us to present ourselves to Him. It is the attitude of Isaiah in Isaiah 6:8 when he says, "Here am I Lord, send me!" The Lord does not wish to do things in your life against your will. He will not force you to grow, develop, and mature. Instead, He desires of each of His children that they yield to Him and give themselves up.

The apostle says that this is our "reasonable service of worship." In other words, it is the least that we can do. We owe our maker. We owe Him for innumerable blessings and constant care. We owe Him for paying the ultimate price for our own selfish choices. We owe Him because we have been bought and paid for. We are His possession, 1 Corinthians 6:19-20.

The call to total commitment is probably well illustrated in Moses. I say it is well illustrated because he seems to have had as much trouble answering it as we do today. Consider Moses when the Lord called him to go back to Egypt and lead His people to freedom. Comparatively speaking, if most of us had in our hands a list of men we were going to choose a leader from, Moses would be so low on that list as to be off the page. For example...

He would have had a terrible self-image. After all, he was about eighty years old. Surely that would be too old to start earning the respect of several million Israelites. It must be too old to begin life over as a leader and judge in a job that would require the patience of Job and the wisdom of Solomon. He was also an escaped fugitive. How could he go back to the land where he had committed a capitol crime? And on top of everything else, he had been a sheepherder now for about forty years. How could he go to Egypt and reason with a Pharaoh who despised and looked down on sheepherders?

He was out of touch with those whom he would have to deal with. Although he had been raised in the house of Pharaoh, he was forty years away from his education, court manners, etc. What would you have forgotten in forty years? He had also run from Egypt while the Israelites had stayed. Not a good choice for promoting good communication.

Exodus 3:11 seems to indicate that he had no attitude of leadership. Forty years with the sheep had done its work on him. Moses did not seem to have any self-confidence or mindset of vision and initiative. "Who am I" to be a judge, a prophet, a leader of millions, he seems to say.

His arguing with God points out his lack of faith. Rather than trusting that God knows what is best and has made the very best choice available, Moses immediately turns to excuses and rationalizing to try and sidestep the plan God has for his life.

Exodus 4:10 illustrates to us that he had an "I can't" attitude. This type of defeatist attitude will never allow one to honestly give consideration to the tasks our Lord has set before us. It is the slogan of the one who quits before he/she ever begins. Moses' change of heart had to start here with this attitude. The same is true of us.

The above five things are also the very five things that we can see repeated over and over among children of God who have had the Lord's work laid before them. They are excuses not to commit! When God approached Moses with this task He already knew Moses' weaknesses and strengths. God is the one who made Moses the way he was and He's the one who made you and me the way we are also. He knows us inside out. Moses thought he needed specific tools to do God's work such as eloquence, communication skills, or fame and respect. The truth was that God could use whatever tools Moses had in his hand to get the job done. His rod was turned into a snake, and his hand was given leprosy when he placed it in his bosom. God simply does not need the tools that we provide and think we need so badly. He can use whatever is already in our hand to get the point across if we will but commit ourselves to His care and purpose to begin with.

Motivation To Commitment

Two people work side by side at the same occupation. One is productive and energized, and the other is not. Two children are from the same family. One makes the honor roll while one makes C's, D's, and F's. Two people sit on the same church pew. One is excited and interested while the other never takes a note, never carries a Bible, and really doesn't know why they're there. What is the difference in all the above cases? Motivation! Different people and different tasks make for different types of motivators. It may be the approval of others, money, appearance, pride, or preeminence which makes us commit to a cause or to a person. The same is true of our commitment to God. There are many different types of motivation.

In the record of Daniel we can see a variety of motivators that might encourage one to give his all in commitment to God. Consider, a teenage boy and three of his friends are taken captive by a heathen nation and marched hundreds of miles into captivity in a strange land. Once there they are placed into a demanding program to determine their suitability to serve. Hanging over their head at all times is the threat of displeasing a pagan king or the

...Growth in New Testament churches

officer in charge of them, either of which may mean death. In this situation they are immediately faced with the choice of eating food, which is declared unclean by their religious upbringing, or facing death once more by their stubborn refusal to cooperate in the program they have been placed in. On this occasion, as well as later in the life of this great prophet, we are given some motivators to commitment. Think about the things that motivated this servant of God.

Devotion to his decision. Even at a young age these men had been taught, and had learned the lesson well, about service to God. They had made the decision to be obedient, and their devotion to that decision helped them begin to look immediately for another way in which the Lord could work in this situation. It would have been easy for these boys to rationalize that they were in a foreign land at the mercy of their captors. Instead, they recognized that their decision to be obedient to Jehovah was a good one, and they determined to be steadfast in it. Remembering our decision to enter covenant relationship with the Master can also motivate us toward full commitment in our lives. From time to time, spend a moment remembering your decision to obey Jesus Christ and what it means.

Clear direction. Many are not motivated to total commitment because they do not have any direction in their lives. It is difficult to give one's best effort when he does not know in which direction to give it. Perhaps we need to back up a step or two and give some prayer and devotion time to determining in which direction the Lord wished us to go. Daniel and his friends knew the direction they needed to go in. It was just a matter of doing it. Scripture study will give us the compass to know our direction in difficult times also. Then it will just be a matter of going that way.

Discovery of what the Lord can do in your life. That is what the three friends of Daniel had to motivate their commitment in the third chapter of Daniel. At a later date when these three young men had been promoted to positions of authority within the kingdom, their faith is put to the test again. Once more, they look sure and certain death in the eye as they are given the choice of bowing down to an image or being cast into a furnace of fire. The winning edge these fellows had, however, was they had already been tested in the past. They already knew God could bring about unexpected results when they were willing to "commit" themselves to Him. This knowledge surely had to affect their thinking in a positive way as they immediately answered the king to the effect that, "We know that God can save us, but even if He doesn't, we are not going to compromise our convictions and bow to an idol." These young men had laid down their complete selves at the feet of their God in committed obedience. And if you read the third chapter of Daniel, you will find that once again, God brought them through the heat of trial and used their commitment to glorify Himself by the mouth of one of the fiercest kings of that age. Learn from the past and use it to powerfully motivate your commitment in the future.

The testimony already given. In the sixth chapter of Daniel is the account of this prince of a prophet in straits as evil men conspire to trap him in his worship. The choice he was faced with here was whether to keep praying, as was his practice, and be cast into a den of lions, or rationalize and postpone his prayers for thirty days. Of course, this man of courage stood by his God who had stood by him so often, and found himself at the mouth of the lion's den. Notice the words of the king though, "Your God whom you serve continually, will deliver you." Daniel had already established himself as a servant of the Most High, even to the point of impressing this king. Could he now go back on his own testimony? It is like a law of science. When we build up inertia going in one direction, it becomes easier to continue moving in that same direction and more and more difficult to veer off course. His life of obedience up to that point had to be an encouragement for him to continue standing firm in his commitment. It is possible that one reason we do not commit fully to the Lord is that we know we will have to continue to live up to this in the future. We may be thinking we'll save ourselves some trouble if we just keep quiet about our faith. The truth is that lions eat quiet compromisers. God gave the lions lockjaw with Daniel, and He's still got the power to silence lions if we will hand our lives over to Him completely to do with as He chooses.

The cause itself. The last motivator for Daniel and for us, that I will mention, is the cause itself that we are involved in. Daniel knew his God was the one true and living God, far above the heathen gods of stone and wood which the Babylonians worshipped. He knew his God would stand by him, and he knew the end result of his faithfulness. How could he trade all that for the hollow, oftentimes bloody, hopeless religion of his captors. The same is true of you and me. Do we give consideration to this cause we have enlisted with, its singularity, its importance, its ability and its power to work in the lives of men? There is no cause in the world to compare with the cause of Christ. There is no "good work" organization that can possibly come near relieving the suffering of man like the church of Jesus Christ. Our cause is too high and too holy to quit on.

Three Forms of Resistance

We would be blind indeed if we tried to ignore the fact that we do resist commitment. We resist a solid commitment to God when we fail to obey Him. We fail to obey Him when we argue with Him, like Moses, as to why we are not the ones who should be called upon to accomplish some task. Whether He wants us to reach out to others more with His message, become more diligent in our fellowship, do more good works, or mow the yard at the church building. He has a task for each of us, you can be sure. And when we excuse ourselves, we are resisting total commitment.

We resist when we substitute. This is what King Saul did in 1 Samuel 15. When God gave this king the task of destroying the Amalekites, Saul substituted tasks. Instead of utterly destroying those enemies, he saved the best cattle and sheep and the king alive. When confronted by the prophet with his disobedience he defended himself with the excuse that the animals were brought back to be a sacrifice for God. This is where he learned, in no uncertain terms, that "obedience is better than sacrifice, and to hearken than the fat of rams." A substitute mission is just that, a substitute. It is not what God desired, therefore it is disobedience. Knowingly and purposely taking a job or a promotion which will keep us from worship or from having a right relationship with our family can be excused by saying, "Well, you've got to make a living," or "I've got to put food on the table, you know." This will not erase the primary mission God has given you in serving your family and being part of the family of God. Continuing to avoid the subject of salvation with a friend because we don't want to hurt his feelings is "substituting." Finding "busy work" to do around the house and then telling ourselves we don't have the time to be involved is "substituting." This is nothing more than resistance to a total commitment to God.

A third way we resist commitment is by running from God. The prophet Jonah stands out as the preeminent example here. Just like many of us, he had the responsibility and the knowledge of what needed to be done. For personal reasons, he just didn't want to do it! A great lesson is seen in the direction Jonah ran to avoid his commitment. In his own mind he headed out to Spain on a Mediterranean cruise, but in actuality when he was going away from God he was going down. He went down to the sea and caught a ship. He went down into the ship to sleep and hide. He was cast overboard, supposedly to go down to his death in the depths and instead went down the gullet of a great fish God had prepared for him. When one of God's children tries to escape commitment, there really is no other direction to go but down.

Why do we resist? There are many reasons why believers would resist laying down their spirits completely at God's feet and handing themselves over to Him, but a couple come up quite frequently. One is that we are afraid, afraid of failure. Sometimes this is the reason. But more often, I think, we are like Jonah. Jonah's task was to bring the city of Nineveh (an evil enemy of Israel) to repentance. He was not afraid of failing in this task. He was preaching repentance. If he had failed, then God would have destroyed Israel's enemies. His fear was that he would succeed! He was afraid he would save Nineveh, and three days in the fish's belly was the only thing which could convince him that this job needed doing whether he was pleased with it or not. This same fear crops up with us more often than you might think. Some wives really don't want their husbands converted to Christ. They like having a spiritual superiority over them or being able to slack off in their spirituality once in a while. They are afraid that if their spouse were converted, they'd have nowhere to turn. Besides, their friends might find out they weren't much of a Christian to begin with. Some are afraid of succeeding spiritually because more responsibility might be placed upon them, expectation might rise. They like minimal attendance, minimal responsibility, and minimal fellowship. They like getting lost in the crowd and receiving praise when the crowd gets it, and if problems arise, they can always slip away with no muss or fuss without accepting any responsibility to help.

Maybe the second reason many resist committing themselves totally to God's will is not very far from the first. It is selfishness. Plainly spoken, commitment will interfere with our plans. It will require time and effort from us that is not always fun and frolic. It will require money from us, and who among us has that to spare? It will interfere with our personal desires…where we want to go, what we want to do, who we want to spend time with. Handing oneself over to the Master means putting all the aforementioned things in SECOND place. It means we will trust Him to bring real and lasting happiness into our lives, and we will quit chasing it ourselves. It means focusing in on the word "sacrifice" in Romans 12:1. Whether it is athletics, music, our career, a hobby, or our spirituality, we will never reach our full potential until we are committed to it, and we will never be committed to it until we are willing to sacrifice our own plans and desires for it.

The Reward of Commitment

The Scriptures reveal to the believer specific and wonderful rewards which cannot come any other way. A few of them are as follows…

The answer of a good conscience. 1 Peter 3:21 indicates that when one obeys the Lord in submitting to penitent baptism he is appealing to God for a clean conscience. Until we completely commit ourselves into the Lord's hands we can never be completely free of the nagging guilt of sin and dread of punishment. The only way to cleanse the conscience is to do what God says, when He says it, in the way He says to do it. This is what will give us the confident assurance that we are right with our God.

Peace that passes understanding. A short study of Philippians 4:4-9 illustrates to us very quickly that our God is a God of rejoicing and peace. He desires us to have peace of mind and peace of spirit, but these things, once again, can only be achieved by committing ourselves to His guiding power. Men have tried for centuries to achieve peace with riches, power, fame, mental exercise, or immersion in pleasure. It just doesn't work. True and lasting peace is only to be found in the Lord Jesus Christ.

Freedom from sin, guilt, and punishment. John 8:24 is the emancipation proclamation of mankind where Jesus declared "freedom" available to all. The only condition was belief in who He was, the Son of God. Many have tried to ignore the weight of this burden on the spirit of man by means of atheism, hedonism, and even different forms of behavioral psychology. Nothing has changed. There is still a moral instinct of "ought" in men which recognizes the difference between right and wrong. Whenever we say there is a way we "ought" to walk, we show the difference between man and the animals. We convince ourselves when we don't live that way. Forgiveness is the only way around this.

The taste of victory. One great blessing the believer has is the joyful taste of winning, of being on top, of victory. Paul encourages this attitude in Romans 8:31 when he asks, "If God be for us, who can be against us?" The Christian expects to come out ton top. Who else in the world can view tragedy with that attitude? This is because he understands that the eyes of the Lord are watching over his life and his prayers are being listened to and answered, 1 Peter 3:12. While people all around build their lives on worldly foundations, which will pass away or be destroyed, the child of God builds on a foundation that has already been proven to stand the test of time.

The pathway of blessing. In Malachi 3:10 the Lord reminds a disobedient Israel of His promise of blessing if they would have just been obedient. He challenges them to test Him to see if He is speaking the truth. Can you imagine being dared by God to see if He will be true to His own word, just test Him to see if He will bless one as He says He will? The promise of the Lord's blessing for His obedient servants is a strong and sure one.

Growth. 2 Peter 1:8 clearly says that one will not be unfruitful if he is committed to adding the characteristics which Peter entrails to his life. The committed one will make every effort to make knowledge, moral excellence, self-control, perseverance, godliness, brotherly kindness, and love more than just words on paper. These things will be attitudes of living. The change and maturity that will be brought about by this type of effort will result in spiritual growth and fruit bearing.

Eternal life. As important as all the above rewards are, they are just stepping-stones to this final and exalted goal of God's child. This is not a special reward in and of itself; it is a cumulative goal. The same passage that tells us we will bear fruit, 2 Peter 1, also tells us in verses 11-12 that these things will keep us from stumbling and abundantly supply the entrance into the eternal kingdom. The same things that make life here pleasurable (a clear conscience, a peaceful spirit, freedom from guilt and punishment, the taste of victory, the blessings of God) are the very things that will help us to inherit eternity with our Savior. Growth is part of this process. Some are trying to go to heaven without growing, without commitment, without tasting fully of the heart attitudes that God would desire of His people. It simply can't be done. This life is a preparation for the next one. We cannot live as we choose now with the idea that we will go to live with God as He chooses then. It is all connected together.

Conclusion

As we are trying to understand the process of growth in this study, let us give a due amount of thought to commitment. Try to find the "points of no return" in your life where we must face the decision to take off or power down. Once any of us develop the ability to see those points we must learn to give the controls over to our Father. It will mean laying self down and putting Christ on. It will mean being controlled by Christ, not by our own desires and wants. But our Father tells us that it will also mean a richer and more satisfying life here and later, eternal life with Him. One place to start is with a commitment to grow. God bless your efforts.

QUESTIONS ON LESSON SIX

1. In your own words define commitment.

2. What lesson can we learn about commitment from John 12:48?

3. What is the difference between a decision and a commitment to a person, in your mind?

4. Explain what the word "sacrifice" means.

5. How can we "present" ourselves to God? (Make several suggestions)

6. Name five traits of Moses that will hinder our commitment to the Lord today.

7. What can help to motivate us toward total, complete, all-the-time commitment?

8. What are 3 ways we resist commitment?

9. What direction are we going in when we run from God?

10. Why would people resist committing to Christ?

11. Can you add to the list of rewards of commitment on page 8?

A SHARING SPIRIT — LESSON 7

The south Florida couple knew they had a problem when their teenage daughter was caught coming home one night with some unsavory magazines hidden under her coat. The response was quick and decisive. They began inviting the young people from church into their home on a regular basis, without waiting on their daughter to do so. They pushed back the furniture and provided games, etc. so the kids would enjoy themselves. They provided snacks and vacuumed up the sand that was tracked in without complaint. Their home became one of the main places for the young people to get together. Eventually their daughter ended up dating, and then marrying, one of the young men who "hung out" at their house so often. He was not an outstanding one to lead in worship, but he was a Christian and a good man. So they were happy with their daughter's choice. After a couple years the young couple was forced to relocate because of the husband's job, and so they ended up in a place where the church was small and the young man was now forced to take a more active role in leading singing and prayers and preaching. With his wife's encouragement, and practice, he developed his abilities and his confidence. Today he preaches the gospel full-time, and the congregation where he labors would never believe the lovely "preacher's wife" who is there was once a rebellious teen smuggling porn into her parent's house.

What a difference was made in the life of this woman by two things given in large doses as soon as a problem was diagnosed. The first was the loving concern of her parents willing to go to any lengths to get their daughter into the right crowd. The second was…hospitality.

Exactly What Is Hospitality?

The American Collegiate Dictionary defines hospitality as the reception and entertainment of guests or strangers with liberality and kindness. The Greek word that is translated by this term is philoxenia. It means a love of strangers. What we are basically speaking of is an attitude, not a particular action. It is an attitude of willingness and desire to share our lives, our homes, our food, etc. with others. Notice the dictionary definition does not say it is just the reception of strangers. Hospitality is the reception of strangers with liberality and kindness.

Modern hotels and motels offer a great deal in order to compete with one another. I have stayed at inns with flowers in the room, cable TV, a bowl of fruit, attractive furniture, a chocolate mint on the pillow, and breakfast provided. Funny thing, I never thought of those places as hospitable. Certainly they were pleasant and efficient but hospitable? Not hardly. There was no sharing of one's life while staying at the inn.

On the other hand there have been many occasions when I have been offered materially much less, but it had the sweet taste of a hospitable spirit to accompany it. Fresh squash pie that was hot from the oven or the invitation to come and sit in a porch swing and rock anytime. That is what I'm speaking of. There is worn linen on the basement beds and fold out couches that I have been invited to sleep in while hunting for a week, but no motel bed ever slept better. Sleeping in a teenager's bedroom or a basement corner has become too much for some preachers as they request motel rooms to stay in during their gospel meetings, but sharing the life of a Christian family for a week and being welcome is an experience to be treasured. Good sisters try to outdo each other, it seems, to make the week smooth and comfortable for the visiting preacher. Would I trade this for a motel room? Would I trade the laughter and the jokes, the hot yeast rolls, or the spur-of-the-moment counseling? I don't think so. These things are what make up hospitality.

You might be surprised to learn all that the Scriptures have to say concerning this type of sharing. And once learning, you might be saddened to know how much people are missing and how much of our growth is being stunted by not developing a spirit of hospitality.

Lessons From The Old Testament

Hebrews 13 begins with the admonition to continue loving the brethren.

Immediately on the heels of this command to love comes the reminder, do not neglect to show hospitality, and the explanation, for by this some have entertained angels without knowing it. Most assuredly the Hebrew Christians would have been familiar with the scriptural accounts which we have and possibly even a few more oral accounts which are lost to us today.

Prominent among those would have been the record of the Lord visiting Abraham in Genesis 18. Bread, meat, curds, and milk was the offering of Abraham to the three strangers who appeared at his tent door. This was the occasion of Abraham finding out that his prophesied son would arrive within a year. It was also the time when God revealed what He was about to do to Sodom. If Abraham had been hospitable in the way many are, i.e., a wave and shout, what exciting news he would have missed out on. The time of his son's birth was near.

Another record of good news coming with strangers and being given to hospitable ones is in the continuing account of this very story. In Genesis 19 the two angels appear in Sodom, and Lot takes them in. That very night he is given the message that the city will be destroyed, but he can take his family and leave. This message of salvation is given during the night of Lot's hospitality toward these "men." In both of these cases individuals were invited in to share one's home that had more power and authority from God than their hosts could have imagined, as well as valuable information. How much they would have missed without this spirit. And how much will we miss if we do not develop in this way? The same might be said for the Shunammite woman who cared for Elisha in 2 Kings 4. Her reward was a son and later that son's healing. Hospitality carries hidden rewards.

Contrast the above generous spirits with the account in 1 Samuel 25 where Nabal refuses to share with David and his men who have been protecting his flocks from outlaws. The record says he was harsh and evil in his dealings, and his own wife refers to him as worthless. After his beautiful wife, Abigail, saves his life from David's vengeance, we should not be surprised when the coldness of his heart spreads so that his whole body becomes as a stone, and he dies ten days later. The warmth of generosity and the richness of sharing cannot co-exist in a selfish environment. Nabal tried to keep it all and lost it all. Abigail was willing to share; she became the king's wife and got more than she had in the beginning. These are not all the examples of hospitality in the Old Testament, but they ought to be enough to show us that hospitality pays a rich reward.

What About The New Testament?

The N. T. is likewise full of examples and directions in this effort of sharing. For example, read Matthew 25:31-46. This is a picture of the judgment scene in which our Lord addresses both the wicked and the righteous. The difference here between the two concerns such good works as inviting in strangers, feeding the hungry, giving drink to the thirsty, and otherwise seeing to the needs of the Lord's "brothers." Sure sounds a lot like hospitality. Have we given much consideration to the idea that this aspect of sharing what God has blessed us with might come back to face us at judgment?

The above example in Matthew does not even consider the many examples we have of Christians opening their home to their brethren for the purpose of worship. Aquila and Pricilla seemed to have had a church meeting in their home wherever they lived. Having talked with several over the years, it would seem today, with many, this would be unthinkable. Carpets would be dirtied, furniture worn, and children might wreak havoc on some of our "knick knacks." I suppose it must have just been lucky for the church in that day that Priscilla was not a collector of "look pretties." Don't forget Mary (possibly the mother of John Mark, the evangelist) who hosted the prayer meeting in Acts for the apostle Peter who was in jail. If she had been worried about her furniture getting nicked, Peter might have stayed in the cell and lost his life the next day. Hospitality reveals a priority of values.

It Is A Natural Activity For Christians

One of the best places to look for growth and development instruction in the church is to the formation of early congregations in Scripture. This is where committed new converts are found. This is where people are full of zeal and desiring to do as much as they possibly can to follow the Lord's directions. The characteristics, which are revealed at this time, are those that would be most beneficial as building blocks for the individual as well as the congregation. These are foundation stones.

The earliest of Christian congregations, i.e., the church in Jerusalem, is revealed for us in extensive detail as to work, attitude, and worship. Should we be surprised to find (Acts 2:46) that as these Jews accepted Jesus as their Messiah and began to have the "good news" in common, they were drawn to spend time with one another? We are told this was not only in public gatherings of worship, but also in eating with one another "from house to house." Hospitality is a natural result of people having great things in common and wanting to spend time with one another.

In Acts 16 we find the start of the church in Philippi down by a river where women were meeting for prayer. One special woman, Lydia, heard and responded to the things Paul taught. In verse 15 she is urging the apostle and his companions, after the baptism of herself and her household, to come into her house and stay. Her argument, which she pressed upon those gospel teachers, was, "If you have judged me to be faithful to the Lord, come into my house and stay." In this example then the opening of one's home was a result of faith and a prevailing reason for the travelers to accept her hospitality was, once more, the faith that they had in common. That Christians should graciously both offer and accept one another's hospitality is as natural as night and day. What other people on earth have so much in common and plan to spend so much time together someday anyway?

Even More Than Being Natural, It Is Expected

The sharing of one's time and home in the service and/or entertainment of another is not just a good work one might do. It is representative of an attitude of heart. By the sincere and faithful acceptance of this activity one shows the concerns of his heart toward his brethren and his Lord. For this reason, hospitality is taught as a responsibility of all Christians and is especially to be expected among specific ones. For example…

Among the qualifications explaining how a bishop might be found to be "blameless" or "above reproach" is found the clear qualification that they are to be "hospitable," Titus 1:8 and 1 Timothy 3:2. Elders are to be "given to hospitality" (KJV) because they are leaders and examples to the flock, 1 Peter 5:3. How can Christians be led to fulfill the command to be hospitable

(Romans 12:13; 1 Peter 4:9) in their own lives if their leaders are not this way? It is impossible. And we might add, this is separate and apart from the need for shepherds to develop relationships of loving concern with their sheep. This simply cannot be done inside a church building at assigned times of worship. There must be a sharing of lives and values. An interesting note for all might be included here in the fact that Marvin Vincent, in his word studies on Romans 12:13, indicates "given to hospitality" means more than hospitality being furnished when sought. He goes farther in stating that Christians should seek out opportunities of exercising this service.

Another group which was to be specifically held accountable to this practice were the widows of 1 Timothy 5:10. These godly women who had no family to care for them were to be put on the "roll" and supported regularly from the church's treasury if they needed. Before they could become a permanent fixture on the "roll," however, their lives were to be taken into account and their practices toward outsiders as well as the saints was to be considered. Part of this consideration was to be their practice of hospitality. This consideration does not seem to have been out of line since, as pointed out earlier, this practice is a practice that was/is commanded of all Christians. Is it too much to ask, to determine if this woman has been obedient to the Lord in the past, before the Lord's people are put to the permanent task of supporting her?

In the above examples of the widows and the elders certainly we should be able to see the importance of developing this practice in our lives, for our own good, for the sake of obedience, and so that we might better able to demonstrate the love of God in our lives to others.

Rules For Hospitality

As any other good work, this one also can be abused. For this reason the Scriptures caution us in this grace of sharing.

It is to be without complaint, 1 Peter 4:9. The sharing of one's blessings and even the grace of service is of no value if done grudgingly or against one's will. 1 Corinthians 13:3 explains that no matter how great our good work may be, it profits us nothing if it is not done in love.

It is to be done to God's glory, Matthew 6:1-4. If we open our homes in order to receive the admiration and glory of men, then that is all the reward there will be for us. Our Father repays only those who do their work for Him. If our hospitality is for the purpose of "showing off" what we have, then let us revel in the praise of men, because that is the only reward we will receive.

It is to be done without consideration of reward, Luke 14:12-14. If our hospitality is in the interest of competition or trading favors with our friends, then we are wasting our effort. Does this mean we cannot enjoy the company of particular close associates? Of course it doesn't. But this passage should teach us that activity within our select group of friends does not fulfill God's wish for us to be hospitable. It is natural for friends to enjoy one another's company and want to serve each other. Instead, when the sharing and service is not out of a prior sense of friendship but out of love for people and our God, then it is truly blessed! Let us be careful of getting into routines of extending hospitality only to a select group of companions.

Back To Our Main Point, Why Does It Help Us Grow?

Hospitality assists the Christian in growth for a variety of important reasons. A few of these are as follows...

We pick our associates. 1 Corinthians 15:33 teaches us that evil associates exert evil influences, i.e., birds of a feather flock together. We may not be able to choose who we go to school with or work beside, but we certainly can choose who we will have in our homes to influence us on a regular basis. The right choice of uplifting company can strengthen us in the Lord.

A good example of service, generosity, and good works, 1 Peter 1:12. We are commanded to set a good example, and all of the preceding things can be seen in this marvelous practice. These habits of life will build one's spirit up.

An opportunity to love. 1 John 3:18 decries the one who loves in tongue. Real hospitality is an opportunity to do more than just talk about our concern for others. It is a chance to serve them and encourage them personally. Any time we exercise a true love of the brethren, we are drawing closer to God, 1 John 4:7.

An opportunity to encourage, weep, and rejoice. Romans 12:15 and 1 Thessalonians 5:11 both direct us toward a caring relationship with brethren. Most often these things commanded cannot be fulfilled within the parameters of a worship service. It is only in our homes that we can begin to practice real "one-another" Christianity.

It speaks to our children. As important as it is to set an excellent example before the world and to watch out for our brethren, it is even more vital that we set the best example before our sons and daughters. Once more, it is not by our words they will be convinced but by the practice of having Christians in our homes at all times. This should be a natural and expected thing for them as they grow up in our homes. Not only will hospitality show them where our true priorities and values lie, what we really care about, but perhaps like the couple at the beginning of this lesson, it may possibly put our children into contact with the very ones who will help change their lives for the better and save their soul eternally.

In Conclusion

Brother Irven Lee, a well-known and sound preacher of truth, passed from this life in May of 1991 at the age of 76. He left behind a legacy of teaching in his books, his wife's books and her classes (in '94 Otha Lee was still teaching 2 ladies classes and a private class), and two faithful daughters whose husbands are also gospel preachers. In an interview conducted by Donnie V. Rader, carried in Guardian of Truth Magazine, sister Lee had the following to say concerning the question…

Why do you think we have less hospitality among the brethren than in times past?

"We're too busy. So many of the problems that are in the church today are simply because we're living in an age when everybody is so busy. There is the breakdown in the family unit so that the family itself doesn't eat together. Therefore, we can't invite visitors in. It is too great an effort to fix a meal in the house. So, if we invite someone, we more often take him to a restaurant. So we lost this sense of hospitality. We have just forgotten how much encouragement there is to the family itself in having someone in your home."

I would not want to leave the impression that restaurants cannot be used to show hospitality, they can. Brethren who for one reason or another were not able to open their home have blessed me often. I appreciated their efforts and they are to be commended for their thoughtfulness. However, using a restaurant for hospitality instead of our home is akin to using dry matzo bread on the Lord's Table instead of the unleavened bread fashioned with love and interest by good sisters in Christ. It may fulfill the basic command, but it's just not the same. Jesus no doubt at one time or another in his travels ate at an inn with His disciples. As good a time as that might have been, how do you suppose those meals compared with the feast given for Him by Matthew or the meals he ate being served in the home of Mary, Martha, and Lazarus?

There can be nothing but good come from sharing your time and your home with those of similar faith. God bless your efforts to this end.

QUESTIONS ON LESSON SEVEN

1. How would you define "hospitality" in your own words?

2. Why are Christians admonished to practice this service?

3. Give a good and bad example of hospitality from the Old Testament.

4. Why do you think hospitality is a "natural" thing for Christians to be engaged in?

5. Give 2 reasons why elders might be expected to be "given to hospitality."

6. What would hospitality reveal about the widow needing assistance?

7. Give 3 "rules" for practicing hospitality.

8. Can you give any ways hospitality helps us to grow besides the 5 given in the lesson?

9. A. There is (more, less, similar) hospitality today than in times past.

   B. If you said "more" or "less," why do you think this is so?

   C. If you answered question B "less," what can we do differently?

   D. If you answered "more" or "similar," why might there by a perception of "less"?

10. Why is hospitality important to the individual and the church?

AN ENCOURAGING SPIRIT   LESSON 8

Shortly after the Civil War there lived in a New England mental institute a small, partially blind girl known as Little Annie. She was kept locked in a basement room and considered hopelessly insane. The only person in the world who thought otherwise was an elderly nurse who would go downstairs each day and eat her lunch near Annie. She refused to give up on the girl and kept encouraging her. She would even leave brownies for her, which were ignored.

After awhile though, Annie started eating the brownies. Gradually, ever so slowly, the little girl opened up to the nurse. Eventually she got to the point where she could be put in with the other children and was even found to be mentally sound. When she grew up she wanted to stay at the institution and help other children, so she became a teacher.

Now the story shifts to Great Britain a number of years later. Queen Victoria is awarding England's highest civilian honor to Helen Keller. You may recall Helen as a famous American author and lecturer who was blind and deaf yet graduated with honors from Radcliff College. When the Queen asked her, "How do you account for the fact that, although you were born deaf and blind, you were able to accomplish so much?" Without hesitation Helen answered, "If it had not been for Annie Sullivan, the world would have never known of Helen Keller."

Annie Sullivan (later Anne Sullivan Macy), of course, was Little Annie. She was the teacher who gave hope to Helen Keller as well as pioneering techniques of education for the handicapped and helping to promote the American Foundation for the Blind. Hers was a full productive life of helping others and not one of her accomplishments belonged to her alone. They must also be shared by an elderly nurse with a name forgotten and a loving heart of encouragement that lives on.

In studying true Christian growth we must consider many things that pertain mainly to ourselves, e.g., direction, confidence, zeal, commitment, and prayer. In this lesson, however, we continue the theme from our last lesson (hospitality) that shows us we must also live and interact with others. We do not exist in a vacuum of isolation, nor were we intended to do so. Man is a social creature and as such we are actually dependant upon this interaction with others for complete and natural growth.

Encouragement Is A Good Thing

There are some aspects of life and growth that are neither good nor bad within themselves. Zeal, for example, can be a fire to motivate us to greater efforts, or it can be misguided and harmful, Romans 10:1-4. The only way to know whether something like this is good or bad is to look at the fruit of the effort. Encouragement is not generally thought of in this way. In almost all cases encouragement is considered a good thing, an uplifting and empowering act. I suppose one might argue that a person could be encouraged to do evil as is presented in Romans 1:32 where evil men give their hearty approval to others who do evil. I would respond, however, that this is a misuse of the term. When one is "encouraged" to do that which violates God's word he is not being "encouraged" at all; instead, a more accurate view would be, he is being "discouraged" from doing righteousness. Encouragement is inherently a good thing where by one is ennobled, uplifted, or empowered to do more or better.

The act of encouraging is not just good because the word carries that meaning. It is good because it is the epitome of God's directions concerning how we are to treat our fellow man.

1 Corinthians 13:5 tells us real love "does not seek its own" while verse 7 tells us love "bears all things, believes all things, hopes all things." A more focused aspect of this description can hardly be found than in the person who believes in others and says so. The person who encourages another is going out of his way to lift up someone else. He/she is seeking the other person's welfare rather than their own. The one who puts the interests of others before his own is taking upon himself the attitude of our Lord Jesus Christ, Philippians 2:3-5.

...Growth in New Testament churches page 79

By encouraging one also shows his respect for God's word when he works his words of healing and concern. He is obeying the apostles directions, given by the Holy Spirit in 1 Thessalonians 5:11. "Therefore encourage one another and build up one another, just as you also are doing."

He is making his brethren stronger individually and the church stronger as a whole when he shows consideration in this work, Hebrews 10:24; 12:12-13. Hebrews 10:24 gives us the intention of encouragement when the New American Standard reads, "Stimulate one another to love and good deeds." That's what encouragement is; it is stimulation or excitement to do better. A picture of this stimulation is given in Hebrews 12:12. The writer there encourages Christians to "strengthen the hands that are weak and the knees that are feeble." Removing stumbling blocks from another's path is certainly one way to show concern, as the next verse illustrates. But all trials and difficulties simply cannot be taken out of the way. Sometimes people just need to hang in there and deal with the situation until God reveals a way through it. At those times it is strengthening or encouraging which is desperately needed.

We should point out here it is not only in stressful times that we need encouragement. We all need doses of this helpful remedy for life. A study conducted in Massachusetts at Springfield College showed clearly a need for encouragement. A group of children were put in a room and told to draw a detailed picture of a man. When they finished they were asked to draw another picture of a man, making this one better than the first. After they finished the second picture they were asked to do a third, making it the best one yet. No matter how poor the drawings were they were not criticized. However, neither were they praised or given any encouragement. They were just told to draw the pictures. Can you guess the results? Some of the children showed resentment. One refused to do all three. Most just got angry, said nothing, and continued their joyless, unrewarding toil. Each of the pictures got progressively worse.

The opposite side of this need might be seen in one man's memory of his favorite Sunday school teacher. Whenever he was sick on Sunday it seems she always came to visit him on Monday bringing some five-cent trinket that was worth a million dollars to him. Then she would tell him, "Johnny, I always teach better when you're in my class. When you come next Sunday morning would you raise your hand so I can see you're in attendance? Then I'll teach better." The man said he noticed from time to time, a lot of kids were raising their hands, and the class just got bigger and bigger. Encouragement, we all need it and we all respond to it.

So, encouragement is good because it is an expression of real love or concern. It shows obedience, it strengthens others, and it is good because it answers a basic need in man for approval.

The Icing On The Cake

We would be remiss in covering this subject if we did not point out at least one more aspect of encouragement. Up to now we have seen the focus of this activity is aimed primarily at others. Do not forget what our Lord has said about helping others. "It is more blessed to give than to receive," Acts 20:35. You simply cannot do anything better for yourself than trying to help others. This principle is true in many different areas and it is true in the realm of encouraging others also. As we try to build others up and encourage them we find ourselves lifted up by their positive responses and the reaffirmation of goodness within ourselves.

It is a divine law that we reap what we sow, Galatians 6:7. Do you think it is a coincidence that thoughtless and uncaring people are often bitter and harsh in their judgment of others? Conversely, those who express concern and care are those who are often the most forgiving and encouraging. Encouragement is good because we are blessed in the giving of it. It shapes our mind and heart to view things in a positive vein and to believe in people. Putting others ahead of ourselves is one way we help save ourselves.

How Can We Encourage Others?

So many people need encouraging, and it requires so little to render so much service. There are numerous ways available for us to grow in this grace. It doesn't take some mighty effort. Here are a few suggestions.

Believe it or not, a smile is an encouragement. A real smile (not a humorous, laugh out loud, big joke type) conveys confidence and an expectation that the person will do well. Studies have shown the parents of delinquent kids to be habitually non-smiling people. By their grimness they convey a message to their children that says, "You're not wanted, you're not loved, you're not accepted." Body language is one of the most basic types of communication, going deeper even than the spoken word. Your smile says a great deal.

A kind word is encouraging. Words of praise and encouragement make a world of difference. The great industrialist, Charles Schwab, once said, "In my wide association in life, meeting many great men in various parts of the world, I have yet to find the man, however great or exalted his station, who did not do better work and put forth greater efforts under a spirit of approval than he would ever do under a spirit of criticism." Would this not have been the method used in Acts 11:23 when Barnabas (that "son of encouragement," Acts 4:36 NASV) came to Antioch to witness the church planting which had taken place there? An interesting response to his attitude is given in verse 24 where we are told, "considerable numbers were brought to the Lord." People need encouragement, and they are drawn toward an attitude that is uplifting and positive.

Acts of love and kindness encourage us. In the book, Mortal Lessons, Dr. Richard Selzer tells the story of a young female patient from whose cheek a tumor had been removed. Unfortunately, in the surgery a small nerve had been severed and the young woman's face was now twisted in a clownish and permanent way. When her husband first came to her room after the operation he stood close to her bed and they touched tenderly. The woman asked Dr. Selzer, "Will my mouth always be like this?" "Yes, it will," he answered, "because the nerve is cut." She nodded in somber silence. But her husband smiled and said, "I like it. It's kind of cute." And then he bent over to kiss his wife, twisting his own lips to fit hers and showing he they could still kiss.

What love and encouragement was wrapped up in that simple act. Not only did it encourage his wife, but I have seen this account told and retold to illustrate various truths. From time to time I come across it and each time it brings a tear to my eye. How many do you suppose have been encouraged by the love of that young husband?

Seven days before Jesus was to die, while visiting in Bethany, he was at the home of Simon the leper. Mary came to our Lord there and anointed His feet with costly perfume and wiped them with her hair. Was this act of kindness an encouragement to Him during this stressful time? The answer might be found in His response. He not only defended her actions to some criticizing disciples, but went on to declare that wherever the gospel was preached thereafter Mary's deed would be spoken of. I believe we can safely say her kindness was appreciated, John 12:1-8; Mark 14:3-8; Matthew 26:6-12.

We encourage others by being good listeners. A young man who had tried to kill himself wrote a letter to Ann Landers after one of his friends had succeeded where he had failed. He wrote," If people want to help, they can. Here are a few things anybody can do. Smile more, even to people you don't know. Touch people. Look them in the eye. Let them know that you're aware they exist. Be concerned about those you work with. Listen when they talk to you. Spend an extra minute. If someone has a problem, just listening means more than you'll even know."

Thomas Malone once observed that most emotional problems can be summed up as a person walking around screaming, "For God's sake, love me!" On the other hand, he said that healthy people are those walking around looking for someone to love. Learn to listen and you will be amazed at what you will begin to hear and how much good you can do.

We encourage one another with our presence. Some people never seem to grasp the importance of meeting together for classes and worship regularly. And do you know what? As long as they see it as some great effort they are putting out they never will! Hebrews 10:25 teaches us that one reason we meet together is to encourage one another. It is a time of uplifting, empowering, up building, and strengthening. When I look at it as a great work I am doing, rather than an opportunity to participate in growing a church, I'm the one missing out.

I am usually encouraged when I am privileged to speak in a gospel meeting with a church. Time spent with Christians who are interested in the work of God is exciting. I believe I shall not soon forget one congregation, however, where I was invited to preach. In times past it had been a growing group, filling the auditorium which would seat perhaps 140. The Sunday morning that began the meeting told a different tale, however. At most, about 30 people arrived for the Bible class hour. They took their seats in the back of the building and we began the service. At the time for worship the crowd doubled, once more beginning to be seated in the rear and filling forward in the pews. This particular group of worshippers I never saw again all week. I can't explain how my heart fell each night to see such a small group, struggling to fill the back seats each evening, seemingly getting as far away from the preaching and song leading as possible. Not one of the first six or seven rows of seats was ever used that week by members of the congregation. Only when the back was full did visitors sit up front. It was almost a relief for that week to end. Don't ever believe your presence is not important or encouraging. It is vital.

This is why eloquent speeches and flowery words are not needed in a funeral home at the passing of a friend. Just your presence says more than can truly be expressed about concern, love, and caring. If people are going to grow spiritually, there is going to have to be some personal contact for encouragement. The apostle Paul looked forward to spending time with Christians and commented on the fact that this association was an encouragement to him, Romans 1:12; Philippians 2:19. Your presence and association is important.

We are encouraged by working with Christians. Once more it is Paul who speaks plainly on the effect that his co-laborers in the gospel had on him. Aristarchus, Mark, and Justus are specifically named as being converted Jews and fellow laborers in the gospel who were an encouragement to Paul. Encouragement is like enthusiasm, it's contagious. When good people work together in a good work, they simply can't help but build up one another. One will never be encouraged to grow spiritually by distancing himself from Christians or Christ's work in the church. Bible study is wonderful, but is it by rubbing shoulders with God's people in God's work that the words of God are able to be put into practice. This is where His Spirit is working the strongest and where we will see (and be encouraged by) the greatest results.

We can be encouraged by the working of God. In the second chapter of Paul's letter to Colossae, the apostle wanted to share the knowledge of his struggles with the church there and at Laodicea. His explanation in verse two was that this sharing of knowledge would help to knit their hearts together in love and encourage them. Knowing what God is doing (or has done) for us through others can strengthen one to achieve great things. Isn't that the whole message of Christ Jesus, i.e., to be encouraged to obedience by the knowledge of what God in Christ has done for us?

The Gentile church in Antioch was encouraged (Acts 15:30-31) by a letter from the elders and apostles in Jerusalem which would have made clear the obvious efforts of the apostles to fairly represent God to both Jew and Gentile. Their faith and efforts on God's behalf in the gospel would have been divinely confirmed in this reading. What a spiritual shot-in-the-arm that would have been.

Acts 14:21-22 and 15:40-41 describe the journeys of the apostle in retuning to visit previously established congregations, first with Barnabas and then with Silas. Both accounts state that the churches were "strengthened" by his coming and his exhortations. It may be difficult to understand the feelings of these congregations if you have always been part of a church with strong leadership and numerous teachers. If you had made the commitment to Christ that these people had made and then been left alone for a period of months, a visit from your teacher and news of how the work progresses in other areas would have been a tremendous encouragement. I have seen the same situation in Russia as we travel and visit with Christians who feel so outnumbered and alone. What appreciation and what encouragement are manifested because someone cared enough to come back and "see how they are," Acts 15:36. To know that one is not alone and the Lord is truly working is an uplifting thing.

Lastly we can be encouraged by the word of God. Romans 15:4 is referring primarily to the Old Testament Scriptures, I believe, when the apostle says they are for our encouragement. It is in the word of God that we see where our God is faithful and will not desert us. We learn of His forgiving mercy as well as His justice. We learn of His grace as well as His instructions. We learn that this life with all its discouragement is not the end of all, and we are given reasons to look beyond the moment into eternity. The Bible is God speaking to us. In spite of false claims to the contrary (concerning the ability to prophesy, foresee, etc., etc), the Bible is man's only glimpse out of this life and into the next. It is a clear looking glass that will not be dimmed or give a distorted picture.

It is a patently false picture being painted in many churches today that gives the impression one can be spiritually mature and confident and yet not need an accurate knowledge of the Bible. You simply cannot have one without the other. People of spiritual strength will always be people who have spent time and effort in God's word.

Conclusion

Encouragement is nice, it is pleasant. Encouragement is good for us, good for the church, and good for those we come in contact with. It is much more than all of this, however. It is a necessary and vital part of the growing Christian's life. It is a need in most people that is filled by the discerning person who cares about others and himself. If you have not developed a spirit of encouragement in your life thus far, please begin to understand what you are missing. And understand what others around you will be missing until you make this virtue a constant habit in your life.

Be encouraged by all that God has for you, but don't keep it to yourself. Share that with someone close to you.

> I watched them tearing a building down,
> A gang of men in a busy town.
> With a ho-heave-ho and a lusty yell,
> They swung a beam, and the side wall fell.
> I asked a foreman, "Are these men skilled,
> As the men you'd hire if you had to build?"
> He gave a laugh and said, "No indeed!
> Just common labor is all you need.
> I can easily wreck in a day or two
> What builders have taken a year to do."
>
> And I thought to myself as I went my way,
> Which of the roles have I tried to play?
> Am I a builder who works with care,
> Measuring life by the rule and square?
> Am I shaping my deeds to well-made plan,
> Patiently doing the best I can?
> Or am I a wrecker who walks the town,
> Content with the labor of tearing down?
>
> ***-by Edgar Guest***

QUESTIONS ON LESSON EIGHT

1. How, in your own words, do you define encouragement?

2. Can one be encouraged to do evil? Explain.

3. Give four reasons why encouragement is a "good thing."

4. The only time we really need encouragement is in times of stress (True/False). Explain.

5. What is the "icing on the cake" of encouragement?

6. How does a smile or kind word work to build another up?

7. How would just listening be an encouragement?

8. How important is one's presence in this realm of encouraging?

9. Give several ways that the word of God encourages you.

A LOVING SPIRIT LESSON 9

Al was living the good life. He had a good job, loving wife, and two young sons. One evening the older boy developed a stomach ache. Understanding how often little boys have stomach aches, Al and his wife put the child to bed without great concern, and that night their oldest child died of appendicitis The parents were heart broken as they began to live life with the knowledge they had done nothing to save the life of their son. Sometime later Al's wife divorced him. Left alone with his youngest son, Al turned to alcohol and over the next few years proceeded to lose his house, his job, and what was left of his life. Al died drunk, broke, and alone in a small motel in San Francisco.

One's first impulse might be to look down on Al. It seems that he could not stand firm and make one right decision. His, almost appears to be a wasted life. I say "almost" because one good thing came from it. It seems that the youngest son grew to be an impressive man. He is a good worker, a faithful and loving husband, and a father who appears devoted to his children. One who knew Al and the kind of life this young man had experienced growing up approached the grown son and gently asked him to explain how a life so wasted as Al's could produce a son so happy and content. The answer came back clearly, "From my earliest memories as a child until I left home at 18, Al came in to my room every night, game me a kiss, and said, 'I love you son.'"

-Bobby Gee
Winning The Image Game

No matter how wretched the surroundings, there is simply no limit to the amount of good that can be done when love is added to the mixture.

Love is Foundational

As we study this series on the growth and maturation of Christians we would be missing the mark if we did not include some thoughts on love. It is love that gives meaning to every word and every good of the child of God. The apostle Paul said that the most wonderful words uttered, without love, might as well be a clanging cymbal or gong. He said that if one could perform earth-shaking miracles, foretell the future, or even if one possessed great spiritual knowledge and did not have love…that one is nothing. Even if we gave all our possessions away to help others or made the ultimate sacrifice and gave our lives as martyrs for Christ's cause, if we did not do it out of love, it would be of no profit. It was all a waste of time. As we talk about zeal and confidence and prayer and hospitality and other aspects of growth, we must remember that the basis for all our actions must be love, 1 Corinthians 3:1-3; 16:14. We cannot grow as Christians unless we grow in love.

Love is From God

The love we're talking about in this study is a love that proceeds from God. In the Greek language that the New Testament Scriptures were penned in, the love we're discussing would have been AGAPE love. This is not love as we are approached with the word so often today, i.e., sexual love (that would be EROS). It is not a love of "kindred spirits" or brotherly love (PHILEO). This love is a love which has its basis in the mind, not the heart. It has its foundation in the decision of the one loving, not the one being loved. Our heavenly Father does not love us because we are so cute and cuddly that He cannot help Himself. The truth is that we are often not cute and cuddly. We make unwise choices. We sin and turn our backs to His mercy. Yet, He has made the decision to care about us and He tells us that He loves us. While He knows we act sometimes in ungodly ways and are helpless to save ourselves, He has still demonstrated His own love by allowing His Son to suffer and die on our behalf, Romans 5:8.

In the plan and action of giving His Son for sinners, God has tried to impress us with the fact of His nature that John speaks of in 1 John 4:8, 16. The Creator has so much love for man, the creation, that John says, "God is love" (emphasis mine). If we, as children of God, are going to be born into His family and have Jesus as our elder brother, then we should be growing up in the image of our Father. We need to allow the traits of our heritage to come out. 1 John 4:19 teaches that this trait of loving is a result of God's influence on us…if we'll allow it. This is only natural. We tend to love when we are loved. Verse 16 teaches us that returning a love for God should be the first reaction to His treatment of mankind, but real love is an influence in one's life, not an arrow aimed at only a specific target. As gratitude and appreciation for what God does for us grows, it should become natural to be more patient, forgiving, and loving toward others. In fact, verse 20 illustrates that if we don't develop this attitude in our life while claiming to be Christians, we are lying to ourselves and others. Love is the main motivation behind God's plan for man as well as the greatest fruit that the child of God can bring forth. It is the dominating influence in the Christian's life and demonstrates to the world one's connection with Jesus Christ more than any other single characteristic, John 13:35. If one has the desire to grow and be like God, one must learn and practice loving.

Talking About "Real" Love

Hopefully, it is understood in this study we are speaking of "real" love. We are not talking about loving "in word," but "in deed and truth," 1 John 3:18. Love has been defined as "doing what is best for the other person." I like that definition. Having two teenagers in the house was not always an easy situation for them or for me. Young people want to stretch themselves. They want to experiment and be accepted as adults. Around our house that meant (for a couple of years anyway) that we had to have some "talks." Sometimes their mother and I did not agree that certain places or activities were the right types of activities for them to be engaged in. Once in awhile young people are going to test parents to see if they really mean what they say. I remember a specific evening when my daughter was seeking permission for some activity with her friends and the key word in the discussion from her parent's side of the room was, "No!" After all the explanations, all the reasoning, and all the tears, she exiled herself to her room in anger for the rest of the evening. Some hours later, before she went to bed, she grudgingly found me to say goodnight. I could see in her face and her walk that she was still furious when she left the room, and unwilling to let it end like that, I called out to her. When she turned I asked, "Sarah, do you know I still love you?" In tears she stood there for a moment and then replied, "I know… I love you too!" That night the battle was ours. Even a teen could see that real love means sometimes having to hurt or stop the other person, if that is what is best.

That doesn't mean that love is always hurtful, far from it. But it does mean that love is always an "active" verb. Love without action is just wishing. Read 1 Corinthians 13:17 and note the definition of love as God gives it. Loves does the right thing for the right reason; it is never hypocritical. Love will "put up" with people and situations rather than "put them in their place." Love is courteous and humble. Love holds no grudges and is rejoicing, not resentful. Love encourages others and seeks the welfare of others. Love is drawn to the truth. Love is optimistic and love won't let others down. What a beautiful picture of active concern. Wouldn't you be drawn to a person who was "loving" like this? Others will be drawn to you for the same reason.

1 John 3:11-12 speaks of a love which is sadly reminiscent of that which is exhibited around us today. The writer urges Christians not to love like Cain loved. Although Cain would probably have responded in the affirmative if he had been asked, "Do you love your brother?" His deeds showed that it really wasn't so. If directly asked about our love for other Christians, most would probably reply in the affirmative. Our actions reveal the truth, however. Do we "love" one another when we are unconcerned about brethren? Do they need encouragement, food, a listening ear, or shoulder to cry on? One of the greatest gifts that can be given today is something which all seem to run out of, i.e., time. Do we have time to serve others, visit with them listen to them, love them? Real love is active love and active love takes time.

Love Is a Motivator

Abraham Lincoln passed by a slave auction one day and observed a young girl being put up for sale. He eventually won the bidding and redeemed the girl. She figured he was just another white owner who intended to abuse her, but as they walked away together Lincoln told her, "Young lady, you're free."

"What does that mean?" she asked.

"It means you're free," he answered.

"Does that mean I can say whatever I want to say?"

"Yes, my dear, you can say anything you want to say."
"Does that mean I can be anything I want to be?"
"Yes, you can be anything you want to be."
"Does that mean I can go anywhere I want to go?"
"Yes, you can go anywhere you want to go."
With tears streaming down her face, she told him, "Then I'll go with you."

You are able to say anything, be anything and do anything in this life, but the Christian looks at Jesus who paid his redemption and says, "I'll go with you." That's love. It is a motivator that makes one get going in the right direction. Willard Tate ends his book, Habits of a Loving Heart, with these words: We really can't live any better than we can love.
But with God's help – my how we can love!

If love is the direction that our God is coming from and love is the mark of a true disciple and love is the great motivator of obedience, then Tate has hit the nail on the head. We cannot live any better than we can love. If we really want to live better, then we must work at loving better. Love will break down walls of defense that no other force can topple. Love of home and country will send men on missions of death that no amount of money could persuade men to go on. The apostle said love overcomes fear (1 John 4:18), the great crippler that clamps a stranglehold on so many good intentions and upstanding ideas. Understanding the love our Father has for us, appreciating His sacrifice, and loving Him in return for it is what activates the believer to turn from sin and obey the gospel in being born again. It is love which causes the Christian to serve God in worship and obedience. It is when we really love brothers and sisters that we will be motivated to serve them also and minister to their needs. We are all living in a scheduled busy world, but love will cause one to make time to do the right thing.

King Duncan relates a true story from World War II in Seven Worlds Publishing of a young soldier in basic training who discovered a woman's name in a library book that he found full of her notes. He wrote her the day before he was shipped overseas and thus began a 13 month correspondence that led the two to gradually open their hearts to one another. Although the young man sent a picture of himself during this time, his pen-pal steadfastly refused, saying, "If you really loved me, it wouldn't matter what I look like."

Finally, the day came when they were to meet for the first time. Grand Central Station in New York was the place and 7:00 p.m. was the time. He was to recognize her by a rose in her lapel and she him by the book he carried. As the clock approached seven, the young solder waited at the appointed place with heart pounding. While waiting, he couldn't help but notice a young woman coming towards him. With a long, sleek figure, blonde hair, and eyes as blue as the flowers, she captured his attention. The young man was so struck he entirely forgot to notice that she wore no rose. As she came closer and smiled she said, "Going my way, soldier?" and the young man unconsciously stepped closer to her.

The young man then writes, "And then, I saw the woman whose name was in the book, behind the other girl. A woman well past 40, she had graying hair that was showing under a worn hat. She was more than plump, and her thick ankled feet were thrust in low-heeled shoes. But she wore a red rose on her lapel." The beautiful vision was walking away and the man felt split in two by his desires to follow her and his longing for this woman who had communicated with his spirit. He did not hesitate, but saluted, held out the book that was to identify him, and then invited this woman to accompany him to dinner.

The woman smiled tolerantly and then answered, "I don't know what this is all about son, but the lady who just went by begged me to wear this rose on my coat. She said that if you were to ask me out to dinner, I should tell you that she is waiting for you in the big restaurant. She said it was some kind of test."

John Blanchard passed the test of integrity and character because of love. Love will help us to do the same with all the visions of temptation that Satan marches past us smiling every day. 1 Peter 5:8 says to be on the alert when it comes to Satan! He is after weak prey. Real love can strengthen us to resist him. It can motivate us to stand fast in integrity when Satan holds his prizes before us. When we begin to truly love our spouse, our children, our church, and our Lord, then lust, coveting, materialism, and the habits of this world that dims our light begin to have less and less power to tempt and deceive us. Love is certainly a powerful motivator to doing right and standing strong.

Love Is a Comforter

If love is a motivator to those who need a reason to get up and act, it is also a comforter to those who are full of self-doubt and discouragement. There is a country song sung by Faith Hill wherein a mother reassures her daughter after losing a race. She may lose races from time to time but, "You can't lose me," mother says. Every child needs to be impressed with that same comfort that is truly the right of every child, that is, the right to be loved, to be forgiven, to be gently reassured. God has not overlooked this basic need in human nature with His children either. He assures us, first of all, that He does love us and has demonstrated that love toward us in the giving of His Son to die, 1 John 4:9; John 3:1.

He then tries to reassure us by telling Christians that He has not forgotten about or abandoned them. Romans 8:28 teaches us that everything is in His hands. The Spirit says through Paul that if we are in God's love then, we may have confidence that things are going to be "caused" to work together to a good end. I don't have to see the end result of a matter if I will but trust God. He tells me it will be for my good.

He also reminds us that the cleansing fountain of Christ's blood is not just a one-time, take-it-or-leave-it, must buy it now, one time offer type of deal. Although it is our Father's desire that we put sin to death in our life, He knows it is a lifetime process. As we grow in our love for God and others, sin, which hurts God and destroys others, will come to have less and less power to rule us.

It is God's desire that we put sin to death in our lives (Romans 6:11-14), but as our Creator He knows us even better than we know ourselves. For this reason we have been given an "advocate," or one who will speak on our behalf. If we are "in Christ," then we have the assurance that He will take our side, He will be speaking on our behalf. What a comfort to know that even though God hates sin, He will not turn away from us as long as we are striving to master it in our lives. Jesus says, "I will never desert you, nor will I ever forsake you." 1 John 2:1; Hebrews 13:5

The apostle Paul was comforted by his relationship with his Lord even during times of bitter, physical trials. When a "thorn in the flesh" became such a burden that he "entreated the Lord three times" for it's removal, he still was able to be content in his knowledge and trust in the grace of Christ, 2 Corinthians 12:7-11. Whether it is in physical trial, the winds and waves of life that we cannot see over, or wrestling with our own self-esteem that is beat up and cast down by sin, love is the outstretched hand that can tighten its grip and pull us through, 1 John 3:18-20. Appreciating and walking in the love of God is step one for the Christian. Growing in that love and reflecting it into a lost world like the beam of a great light is step two. That can only be accomplished one person at a time. Please let me note here. Until we are able to break down the great and wonderful picture of God's salvation for man into the individual effect on each person (including myself), we will never be able to appreciate the power of love. When this world is over, our mighty Savior will have saved uncounted millions…one soul at a time. That is how love works, one moment, one soul at a time.

Eric Butterworth writes of a college sociology professor who had his class go into the Baltimore slums to gather case histories of 200 young boys. They were asked to evaluate each boy's future and in every case the student wrote, "He hasn't got a chance." Twenty-five years later another sociology teacher came across the study and he had his students do a follow-up project on the boys. They found that 20 of the boys had died or moved away. Of the 180 left, 176 had achieved more than ordinary success as lawyers, doctors, and businessmen. The professor was astounded and decided to pursue the matter. Each of the men was asked, "How do you account for your success?" and in each case the reply came back with feeling, "There was a teacher."

That single teacher was still alive so the professor sought the elderly lady out to ask her what magic formula she had used to pull these boys out of the slum into successful achievement. The teacher's eyes sparkled and her lips broke into a gentle smile when she told the professor, "It's really very simple; I loved those boys."

Love is a comforter that can almost drag one through trial and difficulty into peace and success.

Love with a Point

If the love of a schoolteacher can accomplish so much, just imagine what the love of God can accomplish in our lives if we will but let it. Just imagine what an influence the church can have in our communities when New Testament Christians start sharing the love they have been receiving.

I'm not speaking of a love that is just directionless, self-serving mush, but a disciplined, faith-filled love. A love that is powerful to change men because God's word guides it in right ways. The apostle of love, John, wrote in his letter, 1 John 5:3, "For this is the love of God, that we keep His commandments." The same apostle records in his gospel the words of the Master, "If you love me, you will keep my commandments" and "He who has my commandments and keeps them, he it is who loves me," John 14:15 & 21. True love is love which is obedient to our God and Savior, i.e., to His word first of all. Here I am not just speaking of obedient activities such as baptism, regular attendance, and eating the Lord's Supper. I am speaking of kindness, gentleness, mercy, patience, forgiveness, joy, courtesy, etc.

This love is the love that has shaped history and led millions to live and die committed to their Savior. It is a love which receives its direction on whom to love, how to love, and how much to love from the one who is described as "being" love. In our lifelong search for significance, each one of us needs to believe that someone cares, someone loves us. That need is addressed by our God and He desires us to turn and address it in others so that they can come to understand and appreciate their Creator.

As you study so many different graces to develop and grow in, please do not neglect to allow this one, love, to temper all the rest. Without this one, the others all become hollow and empty motions. Grow in the knowledge of the word of God. Grow in understanding the love that God has shown and continues to show in His everlasting mercy and grace. And then grow in caring for and being active in your concern for brothers and sisters in the Lord as well as for the souls of men wandering in a dark and sinful world.

Conclusion

After all these thoughts on love we are still faced with one more aspect of it. We must still try to answer the question, "How do I become more loving?" Knowing the importance of love and seeing its effect is marvelous and often enjoyable. But how shall we change our character to appropriate more of the blessings of this virtue into our lives? Here are a few examples to give direction to this effort.

1. There must be desire. As touched on above, the knowledge of love is not love. Although knowledge of some facts may influence us or motivate us, knowledge alone will not change a person's character. This is evidenced by the number of people we are acquainted with who "know" they should be making some type of change in their lives, but don't. One who is warned to stop smoking or to change his diet for health reasons falls into this category. One who knows his lifestyle is self-destructive but continues in his path, whether it is the path of drug use or immorality is part of this category. Knowledge does not change us, only the desire to change will put us on the right road.

This is the danger which Christians often get themselves into with other areas besides love. They think because they have the knowledge of the subject they are right, safe, and strong enough to resist Satan. It is not until after they have fallen that they wake up and see they really were not prepared at all. Their faith was a hollow shell, not the mighty wall they imagined. It is much like someone preparing for Olympic Power Lifting competition by reading books about weightlifting. Knowledge is wonderful, but we must have a real desire to make some changes and be a different person.

2. There must be accurate knowledge. Desire is useless without knowledge. In fact, desire by itself, without the facts about the situation, is nothing more than a wish. Many Christians "wish" they were more loving, but how many are ready to go get the facts they need and make the changes. And I stress the terms "facts" and "accurate" knowledge. One problem we have today is that people want to make up their own definitions and standards. To be more loving we must go to the one who "is love." We must accept His teaching and conform to His definitions.

3. There must be example, i.e., activity. When we deal with changing our character there is often a strong resistance manifested in attitude. This is due to the fact that character change is attitude change. A mistake which is often made is waiting until our attitude falls in line before we take action. This will hardly ever happen. There must be some activity without waiting for attitude to change. An example might be the visiting of those who are infirm and shut-in. Perhaps this is not high on our list of desirable ways to spend a day. Recognizing the need and importance of a visit to one such as this only compounds the problem, because now feelings of guilt are added to the resistance in going. This definitely doesn't sound like the way to build a positive, joyful attitude of service, i.e., on guilt. The answer is not to just wait until that attitude changes on its own, but instead, get busy and help it change. Don't reason it out in your head and rationalize – just get up and go. Set yourself a pattern of going and visiting and be determined to stick with it whether you "feel" like it or not. It generally doesn't take too long before right actions start to generate right attitudes. Doing what we know is right can change our character for the better including the aspect of making us love better. That's one reason why the Scriptures emphasize it, James 4:16.

4. *There must be time.* Character doesn't change overnight. Rome wasn't built in a day and neither are we. The apostle Paul saw Jesus in a vision and immediately, instantly, on the spot, changed his focus. But before he was given his great ministry, he spent over three years growing, Galatians 1:17-18. I say "growing" because he does not include his time in Arabia, etc., in his teaching efforts recounted in Acts 26:20. This is about the same length time Jesus spent with the original 12 apostles. Even with Jesus as a personal tutor, it takes time to change character. Don't give up on yourself or others before the Lord does.

5. Lastly, *we must work on ourselves, not just wait for God to do it*. Jesus did not miraculously change the character of the apostles, those foundation stones for the saved in ages to come. He changed them by instruction and His presence in their lives. Those who are praying fervently for Jesus to change them some how just because they're asking, need to shut up, get up, and grow up. Jesus has spoken and still speaks through the pages of Scripture inspired by the Holy Spirit and preserved by the providence of God in almost flawless form. Sometimes we need to "shut up," that is, quit asking and talking to God long enough to listen to His word. We need to "get up" off our knees (and other parts of our anatomy), roll up our sleeves, and go to work on ourselves, rooting out the weakness and sin. And we need to "grow up" and see that growth in this area as well as any other is accomplished by action, by

"practice" (Hebrews 5:14), not by God miraculously and effortlessly changing us.

Do you really want to be more loving? Then love more! Let God instruct you through the Scripture given by the Spirit. Let Christ inspire you as He sets the example of love in His coming, His life and death, and His promises. And then look for opportunities to do what you know is right. Love more.

"Everybody can be great...because anybody can serve. You don't have to have a college degree to serve. You don't have to make your subject and verb agree to serve. You only need a heart full of grace. A soul generated by love."

--Martin Luther King, Jr.

"But now abide faith, hope, love, these three; but the greatest of these is love."

--1 Corinthians 13:13

QUESTIONS ON LESSON NINE

1. Why might we consider love as being "foundational" to all else we do as Christians?

2. To what degree do the Scriptures teach that our God is a God of love?

3. To what degree should we incorporate love into our actions?

...Growth in New Testament churches   *page 99*

4. What characteristics of real love come to your mind to distinguish it from a hypocritical love?

5. How do we tell Jesus, "I love you"?

6. In your mind, how does love defeat fear?

7. How does love help one to resist Satan?

8. Please explain love as a basic human need?

9. In what areas of life can love have its effect?

10. Where does "real love" get its guidance and direction from?

LESSON 10 — A STEADFAST SPIRIT

Over a hundred years ago, crossing the Atlantic from England was a risky business at best. On one particular voyage two children died aboard ship from drinking contaminated milk. An inventor, Gail Borden, happened to be on that ship, and he determined to come up with a means of preserving milk for sea passage to prevent it from becoming toxic. It took him many attempts and much experimentation, but he found his solution, and today you can still find Borden's condensed milk on the supermarket shelves. Borden's gravestone reads, "I tried and failed. I tried again and again and succeeded."

Persistence, perseverance, steadfastness at the task is what we are speaking of, and this ability to endure is the stuff that progress is made of. What if the scientists at NASA had quit with thirty nine failed experiments for their water displacement formula? We all would have missed out on WD-40, that miracle spray lube. What if Michael Jordan had taken seriously his being cut from his high school basketball team? Get my drift? Persistence is where the reward is, and this is true in spiritual things also. For one to grow and make progress as a child of God one must learn to be persistent and stick with the job.

Giving Up Is Not a New Phenomenon

The Hebrew Christians were having great difficulty remaining faithful. The beginning of the Hebrew congregation was impressive as we read of 3,000 being baptized the first day (Acts 2:41) and that number soon swelling to over 5,000 men (Acts 4:4). Over the next several years, however, that wonderful momentum slows as does personal growth in the church. Hebrews 5:11-14 chronicles the fact that individuals in the church should have grown to the point of teaching others. Instead, it was necessary that they keep reviewing elementary principles. Chapter ten tells us that in the early days of the church these Christians had endured great sufferings, not only by becoming public spectacles themselves but also by taking the side of those who were being persecuted, vv. 32-35. This is probably the same Jewish persecution begun in Acts 8 with the martyrdom of Stephen that resulted in the great dispersion. The encouragement from the Holy Spirit in 10:36 is that these saints needed endurance. Verse 39 teaches that this loss of endurance, this "shrinking back" will eventually lead one to lose his salvation.

Whether it is in the first century or the twentieth, God's people need endurance in order to grow and mature. Through good times and times of trial Christians need to persevere and remain steadfast in the way of truth. Samson labored with the women grinding corn, blind and weakened by his own failure (and guilt?) without giving up. Because he persevered in his trust of God, however, his opportunity came and he was able to kill more of his enemies at his own death than in all his life. Jesus endured, desiring to "pass" on the torment before Him, yet persevering in His obedience until the moment he cried, "It is finished." For opportunity, for obedience, for reward, steadfastness is the key.

Five Things That Hinder Steadfastness

Just as the endurance of the Hebrew Christians was waning, so also our perseverance will weaken if we are not cautious to keep it firm. The same tools that Satan used against those brethren will likewise slow our growth and lead us toward destruction. For example...

In the first three chapters of the Hebrew letter they are reminded that Christ cannot be put into second place; not behind angels, not behind this world, and not behind Moses and/or the Old Law. Jesus will not share our minds and hearts with anything. He desires the preeminence. When we allow other interests to take first place, then our spiritual lives will suffer. Steadfastness will suffer if we give our best time and effort to the world. One way we can be objective in discovering where our priorities lie is to be objective in answering a few questions. Where do I spend my money? How much do I spend on my recreations compared to my contribution? Where do I spend my free time? Once more, how does time spent on self compare to hours in the Lord's service? Don't be hasty in answering these questions. One adult Bible class in a large congregation jokingly accepted a questionnaire detailing expenses in money and time on God and self. The joke took a more serious turn the following Sunday when class assembled with questions answered and a more sober outlook in the minds of some class members when they saw where their priorities really were at. A couple got so insulted that they just refused to finish the survey. If preaching and teaching in Russia has taught me one thing, it is that in our society we take a great many luxuries for granted as we struggle to give God the leftovers. Some more questions would be, where do my companions come from and do I spend more time with Christian associations or non-Christians? Steadfastness to Christ demands that we make time in our lives for Him and His people.

Even the one who is doing good is in danger. Hebrews 4 begins with a warning about stopping to rest while in this life. We cannot ever forget that our rest is yet ahead of us. When we stop to look at what we've done, we are in danger of drifting. Many have stopped to admire their good works on God's behalf, only to fail to get moving again. It is almost impossible to make any forward progress when we are looking backward. Our rest is later. We need endurance now.

In Hebrews 5 there is admonition about acting upon what we know. Verse eleven especially points out "dullness" of spiritual hearing to be a result of not acting upon the knowledge we have. For example, if we know our tongues are dangerous, why do we not bridle them? If study is demanded, why do so many fail to do so? The list could go on and on, but the point remains the same. If we are not willing to do what we already know to do, how can we ever expect to grow into that which we may not understand presently? Jesus reminds us that the one who is faithful in a very little thing will be faithful in much, and the one who is unfaithful in a very little thing will be unfaithful in much. There is no use deceiving ourselves about great works we would do for God in the future if we will not work on the small things now that we know we should be doing.

The sixth chapter points to the danger of continuing to lay those elementary foundations without pushing forward. We do not build and rebuild foundations upon foundations when we are building a home. We do not build a foundation and then move in to live there. Foundations are for putting a finished building on. Sooner or later we must press on past the basic obedience of the gospel to teaching others, dealing with insincere people, or carrying the burdens of brethren weighed down by the cares of life. When we fail to stretch ourselves and take on new challenges on the Lord's behalf, then we inhibit our growth. When we fail to extend ourselves spiritually, then we lose strength and our endurance suffers.

Lastly, Hebrews 7 and 8 reveal a serious problem to one's perseverance. It has to do with failing to appreciate the high priesthood of our Master. One simply cannot summon the love and passion to remain dedicated without understanding the sacrifice of Jesus, His mediatorship, and His everlasting life that He shares with us. Due time ought to be spent in developing an appreciation for the love that has been shown to men in the giving of an innocent man as redemption for the guilty. Once again, this is an area in which Satan seeks to manipulate us by keeping us so busy with this task or that one, that we don't give Jesus the appreciation He deserves. It is necessary that we slow down regularly and contemplate what God had done and what our Lord continues to do on our behalf. Some of my most humbling considerations have come to me in the quiet splendor of the autumn woods. Passing hours on a deer stand while waiting to ambush the "great stag of the woods" can be a growth experience if one recognizes the value in spending time with one's own thoughts and counting the blessings that our Creator has given us. Find your own time of contemplation wherein you can build appreciation for the Lord that will help you persevere in more difficult times. Your meditation time may be during a brisk walk each evening or on your knees each morning, but a regular time of prayer, thanksgiving, and contemplation is an important part of becoming steadfast.

These five aforementioned things can weaken our persistence as they did the Hebrew saints, i.e.,
1. Putting Jesus into second place in our lives
2. Stopping to rest and look back too much
3. Failing to practice what we already know to be true
4. Rebuilding foundations instead of building the building upward for its purpose
5. Failing to appreciate the high priesthood of Jesus

But being aware of the Devil's schemes (2 Corinthians 2:11) is the first step in defeating him. We should be able to focus past the above stumbling blocks and heed the apostle Paul's words in 1 Corinthians 15:58, "Be ye steadfast, immovable, always abounding in the work of the Lord." What Paul calls steadfastness here, Peter calls perseverance in 2 Peter 1:6 and says we should be adding this into our life. Let me encourage you to add a healthy dose of steadfastness to your spirituality. You might add it to your…

Faith

This is exactly the point of 2 Peter 1:6 which tells us that perseverance is not necessarily a trait which one is born with, but a virtue to be cultivated and developed. Peter goes on to say that this is one of those qualities which, if it is increasing, will help us to be fruitful and useful with the knowledge of Christ, verse 8. To ignore this aspect of our character is to be spiritually blind or short-sighted, verse 9. We need steadfastness in our faith to continue trusting in God even when we cannot see the end of a matter.

A good example of this might be seen in one of the most heart-rending situations a human being has to face, that is, the death of a loved one. It is not uncommon to hear statements at funerals questioning and even blaming God for the loss. Again, it is sad, but not uncommon to hear of believers who even go so far as to turn their backs upon God, blaming Him for their grief. 2 Samuel 12 gives a different picture than this with the account of David, a man of great faith. As a result of his sin, God takes David's child from him with sickness. The Bible records David praying, fasting, and mourning for the child for a week, but the son died. Without missing a beat, it seems, David arises to eat and wash and worship. David's faith was so unshakable in God he knew his next opportunity to see the child must be at his own death; no blame, no blasphemy, just acceptance that all was in the hand of God, and likewise, towards God is the direction in which we must all look.

Worship

A steadfastness in faith will reveal itself in a steadfastness in worship. After all, worship is simply the adoration and glory which God deserves. One with trust and belief in Him will offer up this effort willingly, nevertheless, some seem to have difficulty in persevering. For whatever reason, assembling on a regular basis with the family of God seems to be beyond their ability. May I suggest that persistence here may be encouraged by viewing worship from three areas.

1) *Debt*. In Romans 12:1 Paul urges Christians to present their bodies as living and holy sacrifices. He is speaking of the daily offering of one's life to God, but he explains it by saying it is their "spiritual service of worship," NASV. It is right that Christians do such; it is what they "owe" God for a grace which can never be paid for. If it is right for God's children to present a daily sacrifice of themselves in worship, how much more right is it that they should do so on the Lord's day and in the ways which Christ has specifically requested, such as with the Lord's Supper, "Do this in remembrance of me." The Lord graciously gives us seven days a week to live. We "owe" Him at least one in return.

2) *Attitude*. I am convinced that one major problem we have in being steadfast in our worship is simply a poor attitude. Attitude is what determines our outlook on so much of life, and it's a determination of how we view worship. Jack Canfield writes of stopping by a Little League game in progress on the way home from work one day. Sitting next to the dugout he asked one of the players what the score was. Upon hearing the answer, "Fourteen to nothing," he replied, "Well, considering the score you sure seem to be in good spirits." The boy gave him a puzzled look and then said, "Why not? We haven't even been up to bat yet."

Attitude makes all the difference between diligence and giving up, and it will make all the difference in our service of worship also. Although it is certainly not all which could be said on the matter, the following three attitudes toward worship are ones which need some serious attention if our persistence in this area is lacking.

Ephesians 3:20 teaches us to give thanks for all things. The thankful heart will be drawn to a praise filled worship in order to say thank you with brothers and sisters in Christ. The self-centered heart sees no purpose there, nothing to gain, no reason to trouble self.

A second attitude about assembling to worship is revealed in Hebrews 10:23-25. The writer encourages Christians not to "waver" but to "hold fast."

Tied intimately into this passage in which faithful assembling is directed is the encouragement to "consider...one another" and "encourage one another." Worship is not only for self, it is an opportunity to revive the failing spirits of brethren. A proper attitude toward worship will include the desire to be present to lift up others and see to their needs.

    3) *Need.* A proper attitude toward worship will also include a humble dose of self-examination. I like the way the Spirit gave us 1 Corinthians 8:2, "If anyone supposes that he knows anything, he has not yet known as he ought to know." We gather to worship to say thank you to God and to encourage one another. But we also gather because we don't know it all. We need teachers and elders and preaching and brethren to help us grow in understanding God's word and each other. One who claims no need of assembling with brethren is saying they have no need to be taught. They perhaps labor under the mistaken opinion that they can discover all truth, correctly, by themselves. If it were true, then this person especially needs to be at every Bible class, worship service, and special meeting. Such an intellect which needs no teaching and yet can know all truth correctly needs to be present to help the rest of us. There really is no reason to be absent.

> **The Christian cannot afford to be weak-kneed and staggering back and forth between convictions.**

Our Homes

    In an age when no-fault divorce is touching every family to some degree, when living together instead of marriage is not only accepted but encouraged, and homosexuals are being granted privileges which put their relationships on an equal par with marriage, steadfastness in our homes must be recognized as a necessity.

    When our heavenly Father encourages men in Ephesians 5 to love their wives as their own bodies, to nourish and cherish her like his own flesh, He does not mean to do it for just awhile. He states in verse 25 that men should love their wives like Christ loved the church, and that's longer than yours or my lifetime. The same principle is true in this passage with regard to the wife's feelings toward her husband. That is not to say it is easy at all times, it isn't. But it is still demanded of those who intend to call themselves after Christ Jesus. Persistence is the key. With perseverance, love can be discovered and rediscovered many times in a marriage. In fact, it has been noted by counseling professionals that this is a normal aspect to long-lived marriages. Partners will "fall in love" with their mate many times over the course of their lifetime. The secret is to hold fast during those times when we may feel we have "fallen out of love." How sad for those in this life who never learn the secret of steadfastness. These are the ones who will quit and turn away when the first "feelings" seem to be cooling. They will never learn the richness and depth of a mature loving relationship.

In similar ways parents must be steadfast with children. The understanding from Ephesians 6:4 is that fathers should be raising children with instruction and discipline. Discipline implies steadfastness. This might mean not changing the rules on a child once the "law has been laid down." It sometimes means standing firm on what has been said and not giving into whining or crying. It also means not backing away from a loving relationship with our children. Our Creator is always ready to forgive and accept us back, and He is our example and guide in right behavior. Although sinful behavior is unacceptable, our children should never have a reason to doubt that they are loved and are welcome in our arms. Older children should understand that whenever they are willing to repent of inappropriate behavior, our love has never stopped; they will be forgiven completely. 1 Corinthians 13:8 explains that "love never fails." Nowhere are the enduring qualities of lasting love more needed than in our homes, nor do they reap a richer reward. Persistence is the key.

A Foundation for Life

We have considered the need of developing a steadfast spirit in faith, in worship, and in our homes. These are just examples. We could speak of steadfastness in love, in teaching the truth, in standing on doctrinal foundation, etc., etc. The principle is still the same. In our walk toward godliness we must not be blown about by every wind of doctrine. The Christian cannot afford to be weak-kneed and staggering back and forth between convictions. This is not to say the child of God cannot change his mind. He certainly can and should at the proper times, especially to turn back from sin and temptation. It is to say, however, that the Christian should be choosing his way through life carefully, making decisions based upon God's word. Standing upon the guidance of Scripture, there should not be a great need for radical course corrections. One's home is probably a good example of this. Using scriptural wisdom and good associations, one chooses a spouse. Two Christians understand the serious weight God places on the marriage vows, so consideration is given, promises are exchanged, and divorce is ruled out as an option. Later, again, the Scriptures are given due consideration. Mature thought goes into it when disciplining the children is discussed. When plans are made, barring extra special events, the course of a few years is embarked on. In both cases, steadfastness is enjoined upon mate and parent. And in both cases the greatest tragedies will arise if perseverance in these goals is forgotten.

Jesus said in Matthew 7 that, "Everyone who hears these words of mine, and acts upon them, may be compared to a wise man, who built his house upon the rock. And the rains descended, and the floods came, and the winds blew, and burst against that house; and yet it did not fall, for it had bee founded upon the rock." Our rock is the word of God and this rock, when followed, gives stability to our lives. Each of us are going to have winds and storms burst against our homes. Sometimes window panes might even be shattered by the tragedies which come our way. But our lives don't have to be blown apart if we will but persevere. Our foundation is solid if we will be steadfast.

Just like a plant that is uprooted cannot continue to grow, neither will we. We must strive to resist all the efforts of Satan to shake us loose from our moorings. For growth to take place the child of God must sink his roots deep and endure good times and bad. He must be patient and persevere in those paths he knows to be right. Remember the word of the Spirit through Paul, "Be ye steadfast, immovable, always abounding in the work of the Lord, for you know that your toil is not in vain, in the Lord."

...Growth in New Testament churches

QUESTIONS FOR LESSON TEN

1. What are some synonyms for "steadfastness"?

2. What are 5 things that hurt the Hebrew Christians' steadfastness and can also hurt ours?
    1.
    2.
    3.
    4.
    5.

3. What is one result of adding perseverance to our faith? 2 Peter 1:6-9

4. What are the dangers of not working on this grace?

5. What is an easily seen test of steadfastness?

6. Name 3 areas to look at worship from that may possibly help our steadfastness.
    1.   2.   3.

7. What 3 attitudes should we access during worship?
    1.
    2.
    3.

8. Outside of actual worship, what area of life can perhaps best be helped by developing a steadfast spirit?

    Why?

9. Why is steadfastness such an important part of the growth process?

LESSON 11   A UNIFIED SPIRIT

A good lesson might be learned from the story of 10 year old Sarah Frager who was born with a muscle missing in her foot and had to wear a brace all the time. One beautiful spring day she came home from school announcing that she had competed in "field day," a day of racing and competitive events at her school.

You can imagine how her father's mind raced as he tried to think of some encouraging words for his beautiful little girl so she would not be hurt. He summoned up words which he had heard famous coaches tell their players on days when they too had faced defeat, but before he got a word out, Sarah was looking up at him saying, "Daddy, I won two of the races!"

He couldn't believe it, but then Sarah said, "I had an advantage."

Ahhh, he thought, that explains it. She must have been given a head start or…   And again, before he could say anything Sarah was saying, "Daddy, I didn't get a head start…my advantage was I had to try harder!"

That's heart!

Stan Frager, "A Third Serving of Chicken Soup for the Soul"

As we look around it is not hard to see congregations which seem to be wearing a spiritual leg brace all the time. Some lack good leadership while a good many lack any kind of leadership at all. Some have old scars which haven't completely healed, and some have folks who are busy making new wounds. Consistent teaching is lacking in one place, and real love is lacking in mediocrity. Is it any wonder that across denominational lines the average church in America has less than 70 members? When a congregation numbers over 100, it has surpassed over 50% of the churches in this country. Churches (including the Lord's church) sometimes seem to be busy dividing and splitting almost as quickly as we can get a few people together to find something to leave about. We are handicapped by selfishness, personal opinions, tradition, fear, personal comfort zones, and a real biblical ignorance of the "weightier matters" such as mercy, forgiveness, and love. Does this mean that the Lord's church is doomed to limp around, hobbling from one challenge to the next that the Lord lays before us? Does it mean that division is unavoidable? Absolutely not! It simply means that the church is composed of people like you and me. They are people with hurts, problems, and misunderstandings. Some of them haven't learned to communicate effectively, and others haven't learned how to love yet. But notice, there is not a single thing in the aforementioned list that can't be cured. We may be limping at times, but we have an advantage. Our advantage is that we have been given a revelation, a mirror, if you will, to examine ourselves. We are running a race through life and we must simply try harder. One of the areas we must try harder in is the area of unity.

God's Church Is Worth the Effort

The Bible is very clear in the matter of the church being in the mind of God since the foundation of the world. Paul calls it His "eternal purpose" which He carried out in Christ Jesus, Ephesians 3:10. In chapter one and verse 4 the apostle speaks of God choosing His people "before the foundation of the world." In 1 Peter 1:1-2, Peter speaks of those Christians being chosen "according to the foreknowledge of God the Father." From the beginning of time then, our heavenly Father has looked forward to the possession of His holy nation, the church. He chose a community or people who would come to Him via obeying His word in faith. When people are obedient to the Scripture and apply for God's grace as He has revealed it in Christ, then we find that they were "added" together by the Lord, Acts 2:41, 47. This implies they entered into some sort of relationship with one another. Acts 2:42 described that relationship as being one wherein they continually devoted themselves to teaching, fellowship (sharing together in the Lord's work) and worship. That devoted relationship of serving Christ is otherwise known as the church. If we are going to grow in the way God desires, we must make it our business to continue in unity with this fellowship which our Creator has both planned and provided.

If God planned it before the foundation of the world and provided it as our means of "belonging," then it definitely is worth our effort. It is probably important to point out the term "church" is used in more than one sense. It is used in a universal sense, speaking of the entire body of believers, and it is also used in a local sense. That is, Christians in a local area met together and joined with one another in serving God.

The Bible is plain in teaching that Jesus must be loved, served, and honored through individual members of His church working together. Gene Rogers says it clearly when he writes in Growth,
"For this reason it (the New Testament, sic) nowhere hints of anyone being a Christian apart from participation in the life of a caring, sharing, fellowship of believing men and women. It teaches that becoming a Christian means being gathered out of isolation into the corporate life of Christ's church.
Again, Michael Griffith writes, and I agree, in God's Forgetful Pilgrims, "You cannot be a Christian without belonging. If you are in Christ, then you are joined to Him and through Him to all others who are joined to Him. Salvation is not…being isolated in a hermetically sealed space capsule, but… being thrown together in community with a lot of other people chosen by God."

The idea of Christians without involvement in the church makes as much sense as Oreo's without a cream center. It just doesn't work and it's not worth a glass of milk.

The Big Picture

First century believers are never pictured as teaching the gospel of Christ so as to produce solitary believers. The exception to this rule seems to be the Ethiopian Treasurer who "went on his way rejoicing" but without any further knowledge of the kingdom. He is perhaps an exception being used by the Holy Spirit in the same way the Gaderene man was when Jesus cast a "legion" of demons from him and then sent him into the countryside to tell people what had happened, yet, without preaching the kingdom. He was a forerunner who prepared the people's hearts so the next time Jesus came they received Him. Perhaps the Eunuch did the same. They "went everywhere preaching the word," making disciples and planting churches. All it takes is a quick look at Paul's ministry to see that wherever he went he left churches, not individuals. Christianity was intended to be a fellowship, not individuals isolated and living alone. Notice how this idea is taken for granted as it is presented over and over in the pages of the New Testament.

For example, in 1 Corinthians 12:13 the apostle Paul writes that "we were all baptized by one Spirit into one body." It is impossible to be baptized into Christ (Romans 6:3-4) and not become a "member" of the body, i.e., a part with a responsibility and relationship to the whole. This idea is verified in verse 27.

As mentioned earlier in Acts 2:41 and 47, those who surrendered to the Lord were "added" by the Lord (to the church, KJV). Luke is recording here the growth of a participating fellowship, not an increasing number of isolated Christians. Notice in v. 46 that they were in each others homes (lives!) as well as together in worship.

In 1 Corinthians 12:7 we find that when miraculous gifts of the Holy Spirit were given to individual Christians then, "to each one is given the manifestation of the Spirit for the common good." The gifts of each were intended to be for the good of the whole church not the glorification of the one.

The most common metaphor for the church in the New Testament is the "body," but closely following is the picture of a "building"! Paul presents this picture in Ephesians 2:20-22 where he refers to the building process as an ongoing one with the apostles and prophets as a foundation and Christ Jesus Himself as the corner stone. Peter agrees with this in 1 Peter 2:5 where the church is called a spiritual house and Christians are living stones. Christians are meant to be part of that spiritual building, not individual stones lying about.

There is also the metaphor of the church being God's household or family. This is affirmed by the discussion in Hebrews 7:12ff on discipline and God's fatherhood as well as by several references to the new birth, John 32:3-5; 1 Peter 1:3, 23. Children in a family can't wander about by themselves. They are trained up with and grow right alongside of their brothers and sisters. Most even learn valuable life-lessons by their interaction with siblings. No matter what picture is presented we cannot escape the continuing picture of unity and fellowship between believers.

In John 13:55 Jesus said that the true mark of His disciples would be their love for "one another." This term "one another" practically shouts "community." You simply cannot express love for people who are not around. Our love is best expressed toward other believers with whom we are in fellowship and partnership. As with all the above, this requires unity.

And if this sampling of Scripture was not enough, there is the high priestly prayer of Jesus in John 17. The considerations of His heart immediately preceding His betrayal and subsequent crucifixion seems to be the unity of all…"those also who believe in me through their (apostles-sic) word." i.e., all Christians. John 17:21 is where our Lord prayed plainly for oneness, for unity, so that the world would believe. When we teach, practice, and encourage unity among Christians, we are actually doing our part to fulfill Jesus' wishes.

The term "one another" is used 5 times in the New Testament. Only the phrase "in Christ" is used more often than this one. This should serve to illustrate for us that almost everything Christians are called upon to do is to be done in relationship to others, i.e., to and for and with one another. Unity is an integral part of Christian life.

Why Christians Meet Together

The most basic and elementary aspect of Christian unity is our meeting together in worship before God. There might be many more opportunities in daily life for saints to spend time with one another, but times of worship and Bible study are fundamental to individual growth and corporate unity. Please consider a few reasons why Christians ought to assemble each first day of every week, and even more often if at all possible. Christians assemble together because…

1. We need to worship the one true God. Man seems to be inherently a being that worships. He will either worship the Creator or His creation. Romans the first chapter seems to describe our day accurately when it describes those who think they are intellectually beyond the need to worship or say thank you. These self-deceived ones end up worshipping creation, perhaps even nature itself. Turning their backs on God, they follow their own path into immoral depths. It is hard to miss the similarity between this description and our own society where nature is glorified by such activities as radical environmentalism, vegetarianism, animal rights movements, anti-fur anti-laboratory testing of animals, pet cemeteries, stiff penalties for harming animals while human children are butchered in their mother's womb to the tune of over a million an a half a year, and homosexuality is rammed down people's throats as a harmless alternative lifestyle. Man seems bound to worship something, whether it is creation, pleasure, self, or the living God. Christians meet to worship and keep a sane focus in what sometimes seems an insane world.

2. We need to remember Jesus Christ. 1 John 4:19 says we love because He first loved us. Jesus showed His love in giving His life as a sacrifice. There simply is no greater example, John 15:13. Really, what could there possibly be which is more important than gathering together with brethren to tell Jesus by our action, I love you. This, of course, is in addition to remembering Him in a very special way, which is by the Lord's Supper. We need to remember His sacrifice, His resurrection, and His coming again. This is the way our Master has commanded it to be done, 1 Corinthians 11:24-25.

3. We need to stir one another up. Have you ever stirred up an ant bed? Notice how they get moving about 5 times faster than usual? We all need to be stirred out of our beds. Hebrews 10:24 gives two goals for Christians. Loving one another and meeting together can help us to achieve these goals. In this passage the writer talks about "stirring" or "stimulating one another" to 1) love, and 2) good deeds. Christians need to be active in both of these areas, and by assembling together we can study, focus on and stir one another to greater heights in these vital functions. Verse 25 focuses on a third reason God's people assemble. It is so that we might encourage one another. The Christian's life is not graphed as a straight line. It is more like hills and valleys. There are mountaintop experiences of renewal and joy. But few people are really able to breathe and live in the rarefied air of the mountain top continually. There are also valleys of discouragement and depression for everyone from time to time. Worship assemblies with fervent prayer and joyful singing are one way in which our Father assists us through these times. Association with others of high character and noble, uplifting goals is another way, Proverbs 13:20. When we are down, we need to gather to worship for the sake of our own spirit. When we are up, we need to gather to worship for the sake of others.

4. We need to gather to grow. In different places the Scripture points out that different talents and abilities are given to different ones. We are not all the same, 1 Corinthians 12:14-25. Likewise, in a multitude of Scriptures we are encouraged to grow, 2 Peter 3:18; Ephesians 4:15; Hebrews 6:1. For healthy physical growth to take place there must be a variety of foods: vitamins, minerals, fluids, proteins, carbohydrates, etc. It is the same with spiritual growth. We need the different things which our brethren can provide. Otherwise one's growth will be stunted or one-sided, just as in the physical realm. By meeting together regularly we can learn from the study of others, their experiences, and their feelings. We can get loving, objective help with our own discouragements and trials. Arrogant indeed is the one who thinks he can discover all he needs to know, experience all situations, and judge himself in all areas objectively with help from no one.

5. We need to sing and pray and give together. Our Lord understands what affects the heart of man and He has determined we need to sing to one another, James 5:13; Ephesians 5:19-20; Colossians 3:16-17. One of the most deceitful aspects of modern day religions must surely be the music wherein beautiful (but empty) instrumental music so often covers up and even silences the heartfelt words of thanks and praise which believers offer up to God and one another. It is but one more instance of respecting feelings over substance. It is emotion being catered to almost to the point where real communication ceases.

James 5:16 tells us the value of the prayer of one righteous man. Common sense then responds that what one can do, many assembled can do even better. We need to get together and pour our heart out before our God.

And we need to give. Not just because it is commanded (1 Corinthians 16:1-2) but also because it is good for us. Matthew 6:21 explains that where our treasure is, our heart will be also. I need to assemble and give generously to the Lord's church so my heart will recognize a great investment here. It will help encourage me to support it and remain steadfast. Giving liberally will help me to avoid covetousness and build self-discipline into my life.

6. *We need to remember who we are.* Association with the world makes us forget what we're about, 1 Corinthians 15:33. We need reminding of our mission, our responsibilities, and guidance in our lives. We often need correcting in our attitudes which the people around us exhibit and which subsequently manifest themselves in us. We need to be able to recognize worldliness and materialism (1 John 2:15-17) which becomes difficult to do when we are surrounded by it constantly. Now, just for a moment, consider how much time you think it requires to counteract the influences which Satan throws at us with almost 24 hours a day/7 days a week regularity? Is one hour enough? Two? Three?

7. *We need fellowship.* Have you ever heard a child say, "I don't have anyone to play with"? Why is that need so great? It's because man is a social being. He needs interaction with others and he generally will get it one way or another. People who share an interest in photography often form clubs to spend time with one another. It is the same with cars and motorcycles and home making crafts. You don't expect to see a Christian with a group of Hell's Angels though, do you? We need interaction and sharing with those who have the same interests and goals and attitudes. Some of the loneliest times I've spent in my life were spent during evangelistic visits to Russia over the Russian holidays. Translators and brethren were visiting and unavailable during the week. I didn't speak the language so there was no one to talk to. Even the lights and distractions of Moscow were hours away from the town I was in. Without human interaction and sharing there was just the cold and the quiet. You can imagine how I looked forward to the Lord's Day and seeing Christians again. We should have this attitude always.

8. *We are taught to do so.* God does not waste His words. They always have a purpose. He also does not require of us what is meaningless or even harmful. All that he asks of His people is ultimately for our good. We are taught in every way possible (command, example, necessary inference) that

we need to assemble together with brothers and sisters regularly. We are not to get into the habit of forsaking the action of meeting together, Hebrews 10:25. Because this is God's will, it must be for our good.

The Conclusions of the Matter

Unity is not a natural occurrence. Human beings have far too many idiosyncrasies and personal opinions to just naturally unify. It usually takes a common cause and not a little effort for people to control self and form a union with others, yet, as we've seen, unity is both a necessity for real growth and a command from God. That's why the Spirit says to "be diligent to preserve the unity of the spirit in the bond of peace." It's going to take some effort, but our assurance is, it will be worth it.

Seek to develop a spirit of unity with other Christians. Learn to appreciate them (in spite of themselves sometimes). Seek to assemble before God with them, to build them up and yourself. As already stated – only good will result. My prayer with this lesson will be an amen to the one Jesus offered in John 17, i.e., that we may all come to be "one" just as He and the Father are one. And that this oneness might help us all to grow up together into Christ.

QUESTIONS FOR CHAPTER ELEVEN

1. What are some "handicaps" to unity which challenge it?

2. Why is the church worth any possible effort to unify?

3. What would be one unimaginable presentation of Christianity?

4. Give three metaphors (word pictures) for the church.

...Growth in New Testament churches   *page 119*

5. How does each of the above point toward unity?
   1.
   2.
   3.

6. What is the true mark of a disciple? John 13:35

   How does this point toward unity?

7. What is the primary activity which brings us toward unity?

8. Make a list of reasons why saints should meet together.
   1.
   2.
   3.
   4.
   5.
   6.
   7.
   8.

9. Can you add to the above list?

LESSON 12   A THANKFUL SPIRIT

Jamie Scott was trying out for a spot in the school play. His mother told me he had his heart set on being in it, though she feared he would not be chosen. On the day the parts were announced, I went with her to collect him after school. Jamie rushed up to her, eyes shining with pride and excitement. "Guess what, Mom," he shouted, and then said those words that remain a lesson to me: "I've been chosen to clap and cheer."
--Marie Curling, A Third Helping of Chicken Soup for the Soul

As we strive for the childlikeness that our Lord desired, God help us not to ignore a spirit of thankfulness for whatever role in life is given to us. Let us strive to be the very best "clappers and cheerers" we possible can be.

"Life" Depends on Thankfulness

In its divine definition of love, 1 Corinthians 13 reminds us that love "rejoices with the truth." Have you ever wondered why this is so? I hope part of the reason might be found in this lesson. Love, i.e., those who love, rejoice in the truth because they are thankful. They are thankful for access to the truth, thankful for its presence and thankful for its effect. As we begin this study we might take note of two things. First, if we would live lives of rejoicing, as the apostle commands (Philippians 4:4) and most people desire, we are going to have to live lives of thankfulness. We will never be happy in our life of service until we learn to appreciate what has been done on our behalf. Rejoicing has roots deeply set into gratitude when it comes to God's dealing with men.

Secondly, we should understand we cannot grow properly as children of God unless we cultivate this spirit of thankfulness. Jesus taught that true worshippers of God would worship the Father in "spirit and in truth." It is impossible to worship God in a proper spirit without having a heavy mixture of thanksgiving involved. Is it possible for a child to grow up without iron and calcium in his diet? A foolish question, you might respond. How could a child grow without these minerals to strengthen his bones and blood? He would certainly weaken and die. So, likewise, is the Christian who thinks he can grow and live without spiritual, deeply thankful worship. It just won't work.

If we are going to grow and mature and live enjoyable lives of rejoicing while we do it, then I strongly believe we need to learn to cultivate a spirit of thankfulness. Does this sound easy? It is. The smallest child with the ability to reason can be thankful. In fact, we can learn a number of lessons from appreciative children from time to time. However, from the beginning of time there has been an enemy to thankfulness which Satan has used to bend men to his rule and power. The more we understand this scheme of Satan the better off we'll be.

The Enemy to Thanksgiving

The Scriptures record for us the trouble which arose in the second generation of mankind. We find in 1 John 3:11-12 that Cain hated his brother Abel. What was the source of this murderous hatred? It developed when Cain saw how God had regard for the sacrifice of Abel because his brother's deeds were righteous. Cain was envious of Abel because Abel possessed something which Cain desired. Abel possessed God's favor. Is there any use in pointing out that Cain could have had this possession also? Envy is given strength when we find it easier to feel bad about the good fortune of another than to apply diligence to our own shortcomings. This strength is ideally suited to one man's common weaknesses, which is his desire to do things the easy way. If it is easier to hate others' good fortunes than to work for our own, then this is the direction in which most people will go without some sort of correction.

This obviously surrounds us in our own society. Envious men have looked with desire upon the wealth which some in our nation have worked for and been blessed with in past generations. This hatred has been exhibited in a variety of ways. It is seen at every national election. Whenever a politician wants to raise taxes (which everyone hates!), all he has to do is talk about the effect it will have on businesses and "wealthy" men. Nobody seems to stop and remember what these men and their businesses are. They are the job suppliers for the rest of us. People envy those who have wealth so much they will accept a higher tax for themselves if it will also punish these imagined "evildoers." It has become almost an everyday occurrence for people to sue business owners for every dreamed-up reason. Absolutely no responsibility for self is accepted as envious people crowd our court systems with their hands out. The case a few years ago, where a woman was burned by hot coffee she spilled on herself, tops my list. I'm still wondering why the judge didn't tell her, "That's why they call it HOT!" and send her on her way. When it is not a perceived hurt of some kind, it is a case of defrauding insurance companies. Once more, envious men have decided it is alright to do this because the insurance companies take in so much money. They will never admit one of the reasons insurance rates are so high is because of envious liars like themselves.

We said the above just to make the following point. One cannot be envious and thankful simultaneously. Giving thanks for our blessings is what will give us a sense of joy, but we cannot count our blessings when we're busy coveting the blessings of others. Envy will destroy a thankful heart.

A Matter of Focus

Whether a person is envious or thankful is just a matter of focus. It is determined by what we choose to think on. Someone once said we each have plenty enough blessings and trials in our lives at any one time to be happy or depressed. It is just our choice. Abraham Lincoln said that every man is going to be just as happy in this life as he allows himself to be. We all have problems and yet even people with problems usually have a lot of things for which they can be thankful if they choose to be. The human condition which we must learn to overcome is how we all want things we don't have. These may be material things or spiritual things, but when others have them, we tend to forget to be thankful.

I've wondered about the envy of Ananias and his wife, Sapphira, in Acts 5. Many in the Jerusalem church were selling land and houses and devoting those funds to the support of their brethren. I wonder if perhaps Ananias envied some praise which was given to encourage those sacrificial givers. I know he envied the money because he kept back some of it while pretending to give it all. It is sad to read the price paid by this man and woman simply because of envy. At a time when prophecy is being fulfilled gloriously and the centuries-long awaited kingdom is being installed, they missed out because they couldn't appreciate their blessings and be thankful. Their focus was wrong when it was centered on materialism.

I wonder if it was envy in Acts 8:18-19 which caused Simon to put his soul into jeopardy when he tried to buy the power to lay hands on others. He had, in times past, been the center of attention in Samaria. Now Philip had the following. Was Simon thinking of the limelight again as he made his rash offer? This same envy for attention has driven men in our day to jeopardize their own souls and the souls of others by striving to "grasp" the oversight of congregations, whether by serving as bishops even when unqualified by scriptural standards or by resisting men appointed to this position with which there might be disagreement. When we challenge each other and strive for mastery in Christ's church it is impossible to be humbly thankful, Galatians 5:15-16, 26.

One Key to Happiness

A great religious writer of yesteryear, William Law, wrote, "If anyone could tell you the shortest, surest way to all happiness and all perfection, he must tell you to thank and praise God for everything that happens to you. For it is sure that whatever seeming calamity happens to you, if you thank and praise God for it, you turn it into a blessing. Could you therefore work miracles? You could not do more for yourself than by this thankful spirit, for it turns all that it touches into happiness."

James says the same thing when he writes in chapter one, "Consider it all joy, my brethren, when you encounter various trials, knowing that the testing of your faith produces endurance. And let endurance have its perfect result, that you may be perfect and complete, lacking nothing." We should learn to look for the spiritual profit in any situation. When we are able to appreciate trials for the maturity and growth which comes from persevering, then we may truly say we are learning to be thankful.

One man who had lost some money in a business deal was reminded by his wife, "If you can count your losses in money, you haven't lost much." How very true her statement is. This man had a wise wife who could see that profit and loss statements are not really the way to judge happiness. One key to happiness then is this thankful spirit we're discussing. Thankfulness and appreciation lead us into growth, maturity, and joy which is able to carry us through the most difficult times in our lives. Isn't it amazing how often the most self-centered and childish attitudes are found in those who are richly blessed. Yet, many times the person who we would label as being "handicapped" in some way has been forced to mature and grows to appreciate small blessings. If we are surrounded by a multitude of our own fulfilled desires, it is quite possible we will never come to be truly happy. The reason being is that we never learn to appreciate; we never learn to be thankful. As has been stated before, it is not what we have in our pocket which makes us thankful, but what we have in our hearts. If we will look, there is always something to be thankful for. Even if you are so bad off you cannot pay your bills, you can be thankful you're not one of your creditors!

God Expects It

In Psalms 107:8, David, the man whom God described as being "a man after mine own heart," writes by inspiration… "Let them give thanks to the Lord for His loving kindness, and for His wonders to the sons of men."

David understood that Jehovah desires and deserves great thanks. He was a man of the hills and meadows and had spent nights under the stars while watching sheep. David knew the lion, bear, and wolf and had no doubt witnessed the power of nature unleashed. He was the greatest warrior king of God's people, and in his lifetime, had witnessed the wonders of God. He had been paying attention. Even the duties of kingship had not distracted him for more than a moment from the continuous presence of his Lord in nature, society, and life in general. His sense of appreciation never dulled and his thankful attitude never waned. This is what he tried to teach others in his songs. God desires our thanks. Even more than desire, however, our Father expects our thanks.

Deuteronomy is described as Moses' farewell to Israel before they enter Canaan. In chapter six the people are being reminded to teach God's law to one another and succeeding generations. In verses 10-11, they are warned. They will receive cities they did not build, houses full of good things which they did not fill, hewn cisterns which they did not dig, and vineyards and olive trees which they did not plant. God tells them they will eat and be satisfied. He does not stop here, though. He then warns them when they have received all these things, when they have homes and farms and full bellies, then they should not forget Him.

God knows His creation pretty well doesn't He? He knows when things go well we tend to think we're self-sufficient. We often tend to forget Him when we receive a multitude of blessings. In His warning to Israel, Jehovah is expressing His desire that they do not forget where these things came from. He expects them to remember Him, reverence Him, and worship Him in good times as deeply as they perhaps called on Him and cried out to Him when in Egyptian bondage. The sad history of Israel is how they could not seem to do this for over a generation at a time. Without the wounds of trial and oppression in the flesh of their backs they could not seem to keep a standard in front of their eyes to compare to and be grateful. Will we do any better? We are encouraged in 1 Corinthians 10:11 that, "these things happened to them as our example, and they were written for our instruction, upon whom the ends of the ages have come." In other words, yes, we can do better if we will pay attention to these written things and appreciate all those things in our lives which God has provided, not the least being His own Son given so we might partake of the divine nature and share eternity with Him. If we had nothing else (which is a false assumption considering the wealth around us all), this gift of sacrifice should cause our cups to overflow with thankfulness.

In Romans one, the Holy Spirit identifies (verse 21) a lack of thankfulness as being one of the first steps in completely turning away from God. A lack of reverence and gratitude toward God leads one to lose proper perspective on life. Speculation and ignorance move quickly into a heart which is not fortified with thanks and appreciation for love and truth (verse 22). Where God is not appreciated, then noble standards of morality soon fall under the onslaught of selfish desire and pleasure seeking (verses 23-27). After awhile, without a spiritual compass or light, even natural, beautiful, and common things get twisted in unnatural and degrading acts. Is it a coincidence that since the boldness of the 60's and 70's when men became so hardened as to declare God is dead (a declaration which said much more about their own hearts than the facts), the presentation of homosexuality has strengthened and grown on every front? Those protestors and "hippies" of that day were the children of the World Wars. They were youngsters who had not been humbled by war, but instead were spoiled by depression era parents desiring to give them "things" which those parents never had. Those young people had never learned gratitude toward their parents, their country, or God.

In Luke 17:11-19 Jesus healed 10 lepers while on His way to Jerusalem. Nine followed His directions to go and present themselves to the priests as the law directed. Only one turned back as they observed their own healing on the way. Ten men had plenty of reason to thank Jesus for His compassion, but only one Samaritan actually thought to do so. Jesus' response (verse 17) seems to indicate this gratitude was reasonable and now where were the other nine? As it was reasonable for them to give thanks, it is reasonable for us also. A more deceptive and destructive disease than leprosy has caught each of us in its grasp. It is sin. The same compassion in healing and expectation of thankfulness is present today in our Lord and Savior.

God expects us to be thankful; and He has, by His Spirit, tried to teach us like stubborn spoiled children.

"Pray without ceasing; and in everything give thanks; for this is God's will for you in Christ Jesus." 1 Thessalonians 5:17-18

"Whatever you do in word or deed, do all in the name of the Lord Jesus, giving thanks though Him to God the Father." Colossians 3:17

"Be anxious for nothing, but in everything by prayer and supplication with thanksgiving let your requests be made known to God." Philippians 4:6

"Always giving thanks for all things in the name of the Lord Jesus Christ to God, even the Father." Ephesians 5:20

Conclusion

Thankfulness toward God must be one of the most sincere traits which our Father would wish in His children. It manifests a variety of characteristics which He tries to teach us to cultivate. To be thankful one must be humble. To realize God's gift of grace and salvation is undeserved and priceless, yet freely given, is a humbling experience. True appreciation must also come from knowledge. Certainly one cannot thank God for what one does not even know about. So, thankfulness proceeds from a heart which is filled with the knowledge and understanding of Christ Jesus. There is nobility in one who stops to say "thank you." I was a little dumbfounded one Saturday afternoon at the drive-up window of a Hardee's Restaurant when a teenage girl complimented me (a 42 year old father of teens myself) on my manners. I politely (of course!) asked her what she meant, and she replied that I was the first one all day who had said "please" with my order and "thank you" upon receiving my food. What was noticeable to this teen is noticeable to most people and I believe God must notice when we take time to be courteous toward Him.

> God expects us to be thankful; and He has, by His Spirit, tried to teach us like stubborn spoiled children.

Lastly, there is a child-like innocence in a thankful heart. Billy Dalton was seven when his brother, Tanner, was stricken with hemolytic ureic syndrome and died six days later. The night after Tanner's funeral, his mother, Beth, was lying with Billy after putting him to bed, as she often did to discuss the events of the day. Billy's voice suddenly broke the darkness when he said, "I feel sorry for us, but I almost feel more sorry for all those other people." When Beth questioned him about which people he was speaking of, he explained, "The people who never knew Tanner. Weren't we lucky to have had Tanner with us for 20 months? Just think, there are lots of people who were never lucky enough to know him at all. We are really lucky people."

To be able to see the blessings of God even in the saddest of times—what a wonderful attitude. Can the growing of a thankful heart like this be too far wrong? As I measure my own gifts of health, education, a beautiful wife who loves the Lord, two children who are Christians and who I enjoy having in my house, and the opportunity to share the love of Jesus with others as my "job" – the times of hurt, tears, and sorrow in my life that at the time seemed overwhelming, shrink in comparison.

If any of us are going to grow farther, we must learn to be fully thankful of where we are today. God bless your efforts towards this end, developing a heart and life of gratitude and thanks.

QUESTIONS ON LESSON TWELVE

1. Why is a spirit of thankfulness so important to spiritual growth?

2. What is the great enemy of thanksgiving?

3. Please give three specific examples of how the "enemy" above destroys thanksgiving.

3. What might cause one to forget about thanking God for blessings?

4. Why is it important to put the principle of thanksgiving into the hearts of our children?

5. Give several real examples of how #4 might be accomplished.

6. Having a thankful heart is certainly important, but even more important might be the demonstration of that attitude. How can a true spirit of thanksgiving be demonstrated.

Try any of these other Bible study workbooks in the LIVING LETTER SERIES by Frank Jamerson.

The Gospel of Mark
The Gospel of John
Acts
The Letter to the Romans
1 Corinthians
2 Corinthians
The Letter to the Galatians
The Letter to the Ephesians
Philippians and Colossians
1 & 2 Timothy & Titus
1 & 2 Thessalonians
The Letter to the Hebrews
The Letter of James
1 Peter
2 Peter and Jude
1, 2, & 3rd John

Other Bible Study Workbooks by Frank Jamerson

The Godhead
A Study of the New Testament Church
Bible Authority, How Established How Applied

More Bible workbooks that you can order from Spiritbuilding.com or your favorite Christian bookstore.

Inside Out
Studying spiritual growth in bite sized pieces

Night and Day
Comparing N.T. Christianity and Islam

Church Discipline
A quarter's study on an important task for the church

Exercising Authority
How we use & understand authority on a daily basis

Compass Points
22 foundation lessons for home studies or new Christians

We're Different Because...
A workbook on authority and recent church history that ought to be taught regularly

Communing with the Lord
A study of the Lord's Supper & issues surrounding it

Marriage Through the Ages
A quarter's study of God's design for this part of our life

Parenting Through the Ages
Bible principles tested & explained by successful parents who are also a preacher, elder, grandparents and foster parents

1 & 2 Timothy and Titus
A commentary workbook on these letters from Paul

From Beneath the Altar
A workbook commentary on the book of Revelation

The Parables, Taking a Deeper Look
A relevant examination of our Lord's teaching stories

The Minor Prophets, Vol. 1 & 2, with PowerPoint CD
Old lessons that speak directly to us today

Esteemed of God, Studying the book of Daniel
Covering the man as well as the time between the testaments

Reveal In Me...
A ladies study on finding and developing one's own talents
I Will NOT Be Lukewarm, with Powerpoint CD
A ladies study on defeating mediocrity
The Gospel of John
A study for women, by a woman, on this letter of John
Sisters at War
Breaking the generation gap between sisters in Christ

Transitions - Moving Through the Twenty-Somethings with PowerPoint CD and Teacher's Manual
A relevant life study for this changing age group
Snapshots, Defining Moments in a Girl's Life
How to make godly decisions when it really matters
The Path of Peace
Relevant and important topics of study for teens
The Purity Pursuit
Helping teens achieve purity in all aspects of life
Romans, with Powerpoint CD
Putting righteousness by faith on an understandable level, for teens through adults

It's Not About Me: Becoming an A+ Teacher
A weekend seminar on how to teach the Bible to adults (and teens) and make it stick, by one of General Motors top trainers. Materials and methods are provided to teach your teachers more effective ways of communicating the important message of the Gospel. Call to discuss costs and available dates.

AUTISM, In the Eye of the Hurricane
What do you do when your child is diagnosed as autistic, the specialists are expensive, and the outlook is that nothing can be done? This is the story of one courageous couple that has set the medical community back on its heels. With faith and hard work they present a story of hope for those touched by this storm, helping their autistic son to move from permanently handicapped to the status of gifted learner.

Spiritbuilding Bible Challenge on CD

- Helps bring the familiarity of computing to Bible class

- Covers the Old and New Testaments in 8 CDs

  > ⇨ CD #1- The Book of Genesis
  > ⇨ CD #2- The Exodus, Wandering, Conquest of Canaan
  > ⇨ CD #3- Judges, Ruth, United Kingdom, Wisdom Literature
  > ⇨ CD #4- Divided Kingdom, Captivity, Prophets
  > ⇨ CD #5- Jesus' Early Life and Miracles
  > ⇨ CD #6- Jesus' Parables, Later Works and Teachings
  > ⇨ CD #7- Jesus Gives His Life and the Early Church
  > ⇨ CD #8- Paul's Journey's and the Epistles

- For use in Bible classes, lesson reviews, suppplemental class work, Bible labs, homeschooling, and gaming

- Almost 5,000 Bible questions in a multiple choice format with your choice of easy, medium, or hard questions

- Includes scripture hints and score keeping... students can retake questions to improve score

Order from Spiritbuilding.com or your favorite Christian bookstore

www.ingramcontent.com/pod-product-compliance
Lightning Source LLC
Chambersburg PA
CBHW071515040426
42444CB00008B/1655